Whatever Happened to Maggie?

Whatever Happened to Maggie

and other people I've known

Edna Staebler

Illustrations by Helen Fox

McClelland and Stewart

The Canadian Publishers
McClelland and Stewart Limited
25 Hollinger Road, Toronto   M4B 3G2

Printed and bound in Canada
by T. H. Best Printing Company Limited

Canadian Cataloguing in Publication Data
Staebler, Edna, 1906-
   Whatever happened to Maggie and other people I've
   known
ISBN 0-7710-8299-1

1. Canada – Population – Ethnic groups – Addresses,
essays, lectures.   2. Canada – Social life and
customs – 1945-   – Addresses, essays, lectures.
3. Staebler, Edna, 1906-   – Addresses, essays,
lectures.   I. Title.
FC104.S72   971'.004   C83-098156-X
F1035.A1S72

Contents

Foreword

It is a supreme irony that Edna Staebler should be known primarily for her two cookbooks on Mennonite cuisine, the "food that really schmecks." Edna is certainly one of the world's great cooks but she is also, as this long-awaited collection makes clear, a writer of consummate sensitivity. In fact, as the reader will discover, her cookbooks grew out of her writing. Who knows – if *Maclean's* had not sent her on two voyages of exploration among the Old Order Mennonites of southern Ontario, it's probable that the cookbooks would never have been published.

Edna is a friend of long standing. She and my wife discuss food; she and I discuss writing. I stand in awe of her, for I know of no other writer in this country who can capture the flavour of speech and character as she can. She has the greatest of all gifts – an ear for the cadence of language; and her ear is true. I think one reason for this is that, more than most writers, Edna immerses herself in her story. Most writers remain dispassionate; they observe; they absorb; they write. Edna does more; she becomes part of the narrative. She lives the lives of the people she writes about; she listens to their problems and they become her friends – not just for the moment but forever. That is why, in this book, she is able to tell us something about the later lives of the people she wrote about years ago.

In this book you will encounter few "typical" Canadians. The people Edna writes about do not belong to the mainstream. There are few Wasps here. Instead, Edna has chosen to examine those tiny, bright pieces of glass that form part of what we call the "Canadian mosaic." Most Canadians rarely think about them; many are not even aware of their existence. But thanks to Edna Staebler they come alive in these pages, not as quaint or colourful oddities but as real human beings – the kind of folk any of us would be happy to have as neighbours and who, in a sense, have become our neighbours thanks to Edna Staebler's evocative prose.

Pierre Berton

Acknowledgements

For their co-operation and trust, I want to thank all the people about whom I have written. For their advice and encouragement, I am most grateful to my writer friends: Gerry Noonan, Harold Horwood, Carroll Allen, and Pierre Berton, my mentor for over thirty years. For his faith in my work, I thank Jack McClelland, also Jennifer Glossop, who has edited three of my books with patience and perception, and Elsa Frankin, whose suggestion ended my two-year search for a title.

Duellists of the Deep

*D*uring the first two years that I was working on *Cape Breton Harbour* – my book about a stark little fishing village on the Cabot Trail – my mother kept saying, "Why waste your time? You're not a real writer, you have to have talent." My husband said, "Stop thinking about yourself as a writer; you're not a writer until you've had something published."

I kept on writing. I wrote every day; I enjoyed what I was doing: reliving my adventures in Neil's Harbour. I sent out a couple of paragraphs to *Saturday Night* and *Canadian Poetry Magazine*. They were accepted as poems! My family was surprised but not convinced.

I wondered: could I make a story of the day I went swordfishing in a snapper boat with three Neil's Harbour fishermen? I worked on the piece for six weeks; it was twenty-four pages long.

When I was sure I couldn't rewrite it again I put on my "newlook" suit and flower-trimmed hat, drove to Toronto, and asked the man in the kiosk at the *Maclean's* magazine office if I could see the articles editor.

"Sure, sixth floor, Scott Young." If he'd told me I could go up and see God I wouldn't have been more surprised – or excited.

Scott Young received me politely, asked why I hadn't mailed the piece in, and said he'd give me his decision within two weeks.

My swordfishing story, cut in half by the editors, was published in July 1948. (I heard later that when he saw me Scott said to himself, "Damn, another little cutie from the Pen Guild." But after he'd read the piece he said, "My God, she can write!")

W hile driving round the Cabot Trail in Cape Breton I stopped where the waves of the North Atlantic were breaking on great rocks beside the road. Not far off-shore I noticed a little boat with a figure swaying at the top of her sailless mast. Suddenly a man ran out to the end of her bowsprit; for a moment he was suspended; he lunged with an arm extended, poised, recovered, darted back to obscurity in the hull. The figure on the mast dropped to the deck. A dory was lowered from the stern; a man jumped into it and was quickly separated from the larger boat.

I was excited. I knew the men had speared a swordfish.

Hoping to watch them bring it in I drove back to the nearest village where a scattering of bare-faced wooden houses staggered up a hill that hadn't a tree, and a mass of fishing shacks clustered round a couple of jetties sheltered by a rocky point with a red-capped lighthouse.

I walked down a winding lane to a wharf where perhaps twenty children, three shaggy black dogs, and ten men were chattering excitedly in the salty dialect of the Newfoundlanders who had crossed the Cabot Strait and cleared the shallow earth around Neil's Harbour eighty years ago.

The children, tanned scalps showing through sun-bleached hair, wore well-washed jeans or calico dresses; the ruddy-faced men, in khaki caps with visors six inches long, wore rubber boots, thick trousers, and flannel shirts over grey woollen underwear on a day that was warm enough for me to wear shorts and for the children to be barefooted. Shyly conscious of the presence of a stranger, they turned away with a half smile when their curious glances met mine.

"Here comes the *Robin B*," someone shouted. "Gotta fish!"

Passing the breakwater that was nearest the open sea came a vessel like the one I'd seen from the Trail. As it scraped gently against the wharf, a rope through a pulley at the top of a pole was tossed to the men aboard. They did something with it that I couldn't see, then three men on the wharf heaved ho. A leviathan was stretched from the deck to the top of the fifteen-foot pole! I was seeing my first swordfish. It was stupendous! The body was round; the skin a dark purple-grey, rough one way, smooth the other like a cat's tongue; the horny black fins stood out like scimitars, the tail like the handlebars of a giant bicycle; but the strangest thing was the broad, pointed, sharp-sided sword, an extension of the head, an upper bill three feet long! As the rope was slowly released, the men guided the creature down to the dock where it lay like a rolled up rug.

A little boy knelt near the head; with a hook he ripped open the glazed membrane of the huge round eye that was uppermost. Out of the cavity ran clear, slurpy liquid. The child put his hand into the socket, pulled something out of it then looked up at me. "Want te heyeball?" he asked, thrusting his fist towards me.

Ugh! I couldn't touch the fishy thing. But everybody was watching to see what I would do. "Let me look at it," I hedged. He opened his hand and I saw a perfect sphere, clear as glass, about an inch and a quarter in diameter, reflecting colours like a bubble.

"Take it," he said.

I still hesitated. "I haven't any money with me."

The child shook his head. "Don't need none."

"You mean it's a present?"

He grinned and nodded. I couldn't spurn a gift. I held out my hand; the boy placed the crystal gently on my palm. It felt cool and tender as a piece of jelly or a gumdrop that's had the sugar licked off it.

"What should I do with it?"

"Take home and put in sun and it'll turn roight hard," someone answered. "Be careful not to break en." I held my treasure reverently; it didn't even smell like fish!

"How much would the fish weigh?" I asked anyone who could hear me.

"Over six hundred pound, I reckon," a blue-eyed fisherman answered. "He's some beeg."

"What does it taste like?"

"Don't know, never et 'em, we just ketches 'em and sells 'em for folks down in States," he said. "Don't fancy to try none of the big ugly things meself but some round 'ere cut off a bit near the haid and taked it home and cooked it; they say hit's got a roight noice flavour to it, loike pork, not strong atall. Americans must loike 'em or they wouldn't pay so much for 'em. We's gettin' thirty-two cents a pound today."

I did some mental arithmetic. "No wonder you're so happy to catch one."

He grinned. "We be, but they's awful scarce." With a saw in

13

his hand he knelt beside the fish. "Want sword?" he asked me.

"Oh yes, don't you need it?"

He laughed. "We just throws 'em overboard."

The fibrous grey sword was heavy and felt like bone. The cut end showed soft bloody marrow that was the essence of fishiness. A man saw me sniffing. "Stick in ant heap and ants'll clean en out for you," he offered.

"How long will it take?"

"About six weeks."

The man next sawed off the head, then the fins, the broad black tail and the fan-shaped crimson gill plates; as each piece came off the youngsters threw it into the water where flashing white birds darted at it before it sank to the shadowy creatures hovering in beds of waving kelp. With a knife the underbody of the fish was ripped open. I wanted to leave but the faces all round me were bland as blancmange; I couldn't insult them by running away. As though mesmerized I watched all the stuffing being pulled out of that huge cavity; like a gourmet in a nightmare I saw long white links of sausage, steamed puddings, buckshot, sets of false teeth, lumps of pink lard, clots of black jelly, and bright red claret splashing over everything – including my legs.

The carcass, washed with salt water, was hoisted on a carrier and taken by four men to the scales. Everyone gathered around to learn the score – 634 pounds – marked with indelible pencil near the tail.

The *Robin B* having moved to her mooring, another boat landed a fish. One by one the lucky boats of Neil's Harbour came to the end of the dock; those that had caught no fish went straight to the anchorage, the men coming ashore in dories that had been fastened to buoys in the water. Twenty boats had gone fishing; five swordfish had been caught and exuberantly acclaimed.

I decided I wanted to go swordfishing.

"Do you ever take people out with you?" I asked one of the fishermen.

He answered warily, "We doos, now and again."

"Would you take me? Tomorrow morning?"

He rubbed the back of his neck and contemplated the water. "Well now, I'll tell you, miss, I ain't aimin' to fish tomorrow but if you gits down on shore by seven in morning they won't all git off without you."

Next morning I was on the shore at six-thirty. All the men gathered in little groups around the stages stopped talking to stare at me as I came along.

"Is it going to be a good day?" I heard myself asking timidly.

After a silence somebody said, "Yis, moight be." The rest just stared – at me, through me, past me. I wanted to run but the thought of my retreating posterior made me stay to try again. "Would anyone please take me swordfishing?"

The men exchanged glances; one of them said, "Well, I'll tell you, miss, ye'd be better off in boat with fo'c'sle. Ye see, we don't have much room in them small ones. You wait round till skipper o' one o' them snapper boats comes down.''

Four larger vessels were tied up between the two wharves. I sat on the fish dock and waited half an hour till three men sauntered along.

"Woman aboard's bad luck," one said when I asked if they'd take me.

"I'm good luck, you'll see, I'll bring you good luck."

They looked at each other. "We been fishin' fer two months and ain't got but three. . . ."

"Ever been seasick?"

"No," I answered firmly. (I didn't tell them I'd never been out on the sea).

"Come on then."

I was going! They helped me into the dory and rowed over to a blue and grey snapper boat. It was called the Devil Diver. The name gave me a tremor. I scrambled awkwardly aboard.

The snapper boat was forty feet long and ten feet wide with a Buick engine in the middle. It had a dory in the stern, a high, sail-less mast from which the vessel was controlled, a fo'c'sle, foredeck, and removable swordfish rig, consisting of a plank projecting twelve feet over the water from the prow and a pulpit, a metal three-quarter hoop less than waist high, to which the long rod of the harpoon was fastened. A detachable double-barbed dart of bronze was socketed in the end of the rod; taut along the rod a thin, strong line ran from the dart to a great coil in a box amidships with a red keg tied at the end of the hundreds of feet of line. The keg could be thrown into the water to mark and retard a wounded fish.

We started at once. That they might spy a fish even below the surface of the water, two of the men, Diddle and Jack, had climbed the mast where they sat on rope-swung boards like performers on a trapeze, their feet resting on a bar. The other man, Jossie, sat on the wooden door that covered the roaring motor; he was the "sticker" who, when a fish was sighted, would run out to the pulpit, untie the harpoon, and make the fatal lunge. I saf on the only seat in the boat, a narrow bench near the motor.

Soon we had gone round the breakwater, round the lighthouse point, out to the open sea, climbing the hill of water that rose to the horizon. I sat very still, very straight, very stiff. Though the water didn't look wild, the boat seemed to heave. The fumes of the engine were very strong; I remembered that someone had told me the smell of gasoline always made people seasick. I thought I'd better move away but there seemed to be no place for me to go. I clung to the bench and looked at Neil's Harbour, now just a tiny clearing against the great dark hills. Jossie, relaxed in front of me, kept his eyes on the water.

"What do you look for?" I shouted.

"Just loike two black sticks, 'bout so high" – he held up his hands eight inches apart – "and so" – he stretched his arms as wide as they would go.

I tried watching the water for two black sticks – two black sticks – gasoline fumes – no, no – two black sticks – two black – gasoline. . . . I stood up. But there was nothing to hang on to so I sat down again, clinging to the bench.

"You might be more easy atop the fo'c'sle," Jossie said, swinging himself nimbly onto the roof of the tiny cabin and sitting on its front edge, his back towards me.

I shuffled to the rail of the boat. To get on top of the fo'c'sle, which was higher than my head, I had to climb up the side from the boat's narrow rail, avoiding the ropes that ran from the mast to the engine. The water was whizzing by and very close. I was scared skinny. I don't know how many times I missed but one time I didn't. I leaned against the mast and breathed the fresh salt air.

Then I felt dizzy. I thought, *This is it!* But nothing happened. I waited; I felt no nausea. I realized I never had felt any.

What the hell – I wasn't seasick, I was just unbalanced. It was time I started looking for swordfish.

How could I know when I really saw two black sticks among the billion sharp points of water that raised themselves capriciously round us? Dozens of those impish little wavelets deliberately deceived me as they danced up from the surface, imitated the curving fins, posed long enough to give me a thrill, then mercifully disappeared before I could shout what I believed I had discovered.

We were perhaps five miles from land and by simply turning my head I could see forty miles from the misty purple form of Cape Smokey in the south to fainter, farther Money Point at the northern tip of Cape Breton Island. Closest to us was a wall of red rock with the dark mass of mountains behind it. The village we had left was merely a break in the surrounding greenery.

The smaller fishing boats, weaving back and forth inshore, shone white, red, green, and grey with the sun against them in the deep-blue water; the snapper boats and sailing vessels from Newfoundland were silhouetted in the gleam between us and the horizon. There were schooners and jacks, ketches and smacks, snapper boats and skiffs from Port au Basque, St. John's, Glace Bay, Louisburg, and Yarmouth, from all the coast of Newfoundland and all of Nova Scotia; they had come to find, and kill, the wary, wondrous swordfish that from July to September mystifies and provokes the rugged men of the rocky northern seaboard.

Loving the sport, the gamble, the hope of fabulous luck, like men obsessed, they had piled up their lobster traps, hauled in their herring nets, coiled their codfish trawls, and become rivals in pursuit of the monstrous creatures that bask in the summer sunshine off the shores of Cape Breton.

In July the search for the precious prey is made near Glace Bay and Louisburg. When the middle of August comes, the men on the masts follow the broadbilled fish to the fertile grounds between Ingonish and Dingwall where the long swords slash and the toothless mouths gobble the defenceless mackerel and herring. By the end of September the roving

17

gladiators have disappeared from the North Atlantic to go no one knows where.

The capture of the swordfish is as uncertain as the weather that controls it. The smaller vessels, with only two men aboard, are lucky to catch even three in a season; the larger craft, with as many as five watchers on a mast, searching many miles from land, may bring in a dozen fish in a day – or none. Almost the entire annual catch, averaging a million and a half pounds, is packed in ice and shipped to Boston.

When a boat came near us, I held my breath as I saw the men aloft sway four feet to the right, four feet to the left, to and fro, to and fro, like inverted pendulums. They shouted something that sounded like, "Got arn?"

Jossie shook his head, yelling unmistakably, "Narn."

I asked what it meant.

"'Ave we got some and we ain't," he said.

There were no clouds in the sky. The sun was warm but the breeze was becoming a wind. Our boat leapt and fell in the swells, a wonderful, proud thing to feel. And all the time we kept watching for the precious sticklike fins. We saw several sharks; we saw dolphins; we saw a blackfish blow.

Then Diddle on the mast yelled, *"Fish!"*

"I see 'im," Jossie cried, running nimbly to the end of the bowsprit.

I couldn't see anything but those points of water. Risking my life, I stood up. I saw the fins, those two black sticks, eight inches high.

Jossie unfastened the harpoon, leaned against the iron hoop. The engine was switched off. We were close. Jossie was poised to strike.

"Aw – a trick!" he called and we all saw that the two black fins were fastened to a piece of board. The men laughed about it but I didn't think it was funny.

"Anyway, now you know what the fins looks loike when they's out of the water."

We settled down again after that and even I didn't stop watching the waves forming and disappearing. Sometimes the boat went towards the south, then straight towards the horizon, northeast, due north, south again, always moving, her men and I watching, waiting, hoping. The same anxiety was in a hundred vessels that searched the sea as we did.

After a box lunch we saw a boat that had stopped some distance from us; almost alongside was its dory with two men. One, standing, was pulling in a line; the other, crouched over, was bailing.

"Must ha' been struck," Jossie shouted, pointing. "Swordfish be quiet, restin' fish," he told me; "wouldn't hurt nobody if they's left alone. Swords be made fer slashing, not stabbing, but when a fish is hit near the head 'e sometimes goes crazy loike and turns on a boat or dory, can ram 'is whole sword clear through a three-inch plank – and a man too if 'e's settin' in the way. Sword breaks off and fish dies quick after that, but a man dies quick too if sword goes through 'im or if 'e gits hisself tangled in a line and dragged down."

The wind was growing stronger, the water rougher; the waves were splashing over the fo'c'sle; I buttoned my jacket and tucked my green cotton legs under me. Around three o'clock I realized why I had been advised to go out in a boat with a fo'c'sle. I thought up genteel ways in which I could break the news to Jossie. I thought how unapproachable he looked as he sat staring at the water. I thought how ridiculous it was to be so prudish. For about an hour I tried to forget. When I knew I couldn't sit still another minute, Jack, the curly-headed blond lad, came down from the mast and sat beside me. "How do you like swordfishing?" he asked.

"Fine."

"Ever been out before?"

"No."

"Want to go out again?" He gave me a sideways glance.

"Sure."

"What's your name? Where do you belong? How long are you staying round here? Where are you staying at?"

I answered his questions briefly, hoping he'd go aloft. He asked me if I'd like a cigarette.

"Don't you smoke?" He looked surprised. "Not many city girls don't smoke." He painstakingly rolled a cigarette, lighted it carefully behind his hands, blew the smoke out slowly, and settled himself to enjoy it. "Nice day out on the water," he said, "though it's gettin' loppy."

I couldn't stand it any longer; I said, "I'm sorry, but I think I'm going to have to embarrass you. . . ."

"What did you say?"

"I'm sorry, but I think I'm going to have to . . ." I stopped. I swallowed. I felt hot; I knew I was blushing. He looked at me sharply. I glared back and cried, "Have you got an old can I could take into the fo'c'sle?"

He didn't say a word; he went right to the stern, came back; without looking at me he thrust a battered tin pail into my hand then swung himself aloft. I slipped into the boat's little bit of seclusion and closed the sliding door.

Then, of all times, I heard, *"Fish!"*

The motor was stopped. Now, now, they would catch a swordfish. I zipped out of the cabin. Jossie was in the pulpit, the harpoon in his hand. I looked frantically where I thought he was looking but I couldn't see the fish. I couldn't climb quickly enough to the roof of the fo'c'sle. I thought I'd miss the whole thing. I leaned so far across the rail I almost tipped over.

Jossie dropped his arm. "Goddamn shark," he said. I saw it just as it disappeared: two broad fins above the water. Jossie's shoulders drooped. He fastened the harpoon to the pulpit.

The boat pitched up and down, rocked to and fro, rolled back and forth. I was sure we couldn't possibly see fins in the turbulent sea. The men thought the same, and at half past four the boat was turned towards the harbour. Tired and feeling as people do who have fished all day and caught no fish I slumped against the mast.

Suddenly I was pointing and shrieking, "Look, look, a fish, a fish, a fish!"

"By God, it is, a fish, a fish," Jossie yelled and ran out to the pulpit. Jack, on the mast, steered straight towards the prize. The motor stopped. We were quiet. Tense. We were close. Jossie held the harpoon in his hand. The fish was almost alongside. "Oh God, get 'im, get 'im," I prayed.

Jossie lunged.

The fish was gone. The rod fell slack in the water. Jossie jerked it back to the pulpit.

Diddle came down from the mast with Jack tumbling after. "Struck 'im right behind front fin," Diddle called as he grabbed the line uncoiling from the box amidships.

Jossie ran to the stern. The dory was lowered, and Diddle jumped into it with the keg and box of rope. Quickly he tautened the line with the dart on the end in the fish.

"'E's on," Diddle shouted, "'e's on," and at once was jerked away by the plunging, wounded swordfish.

We watched him go. Without the steadying drive of the motor, the *Devil Diver* was seesawing madly. I clung to the mast. Jossie grinned at me as he passed on his way to the pulpit to put a new dart in the pole. Jack started the motor and we were moving again. Jossie's place on the front of the fo'c'sle was constantly splashed as we plunged into deepening waves.

"Worst swell I ever were out in," he said as he moved back and sat beside me.

"What are we going to do now?" I asked him.

"Look for another fish till Diddle gits that one played out."

We didn't go far from Diddle; except when he was hidden by waves we always kept him in sight. He stood in the little dory, pulling in line and letting it out as the swordfish tried to escape him by riding him round in the sea.

"Looks like 'e might be a big one," Jossie said when we'd circled for almost an hour. He seldom watched the water for another fish: he kept turning anxious glances towards the yellow dory. "Sometimes we loses a fish," he said. "Sometimes it takes three-four hours to tire out a big one. Sometimes a fish will turn on a dory before 'e dies."

As we kept moving east, south, west, and north, all the other fishing boats were going in one direction, all going towards a harbour. Soon we were alone on the ocean with the little yellow dory. The hill of water towards the horizon seemed steeper than it had in the morning. The land seemed farther away.

"Wind's right nardly now," Jossie said.

It was useless to pretend we were looking for another fish: we kept our eyes on Diddle. He was pulling in the line, letting it out, pulling it in, letting it out as he stood in the little boat.

For another lonely hour we circled.

Then Diddle raised his arm. We rushed to the dory heaving up and down in the waves. Diddle was smiling broadly. The water around him was red, the great curved tail of the swordfish securely tied to the thwart.

Diddle clambered into the *Diver*. With the help of a tackle the fish was hauled aboard. It stretched across the full width of the boat with its head running up the side, its sword above the gunwale. "Not the biggest one I ever seen in my life," was the first comment Jossie made, "but 'e'll go seven hundred pound." He thumped Diddle's shoulder with joy.

"'E was a dirty little bastard," Diddle said, "wouldn't go up or down, kep' hittin' the rope with 'is tail." He was grinning. Jossie was grinning too and so were Jack and I.

"You's lucky,'' Diddle said to me. "You can git a ship any time now. Jesus Christ, they'll all be beggin' ye to go with them!"

They hauled in the dory, the men climbed the mast, Jossie sat on the engine door, I sat on the bench. The *Devil Diver* leaped towards the harbour.

We rode straight up to the fish dock. A crowd was there to see. Jossie fastened a rope round the swordfish tail and the men on the wharf pulled it up.

"Oooooo, a good one, a good one," everyone said in a way that was almost a cheer. For a blessed moment the great fish hung high, then they let it down with a plop.

As we followed it over the rail, Diddle announced in his booming voice, "This girl's good luck, we want her to ship with we. Everybody else can't have her."

Maclean's, July 15, 1948

☆   ☆   ☆   ☆   ☆

Though I often went back to Neil's Harbour I never went swordfishing again with Diddle, Jossie, and Jack. In 1968 the swordfish was declared to be contaminated with mercury. The fishermen's favourite sport was over; they sold their snapper boats and tamely went out after cod, mackerel, haddock, and lobster, complaining bitterly that fishing was poor because the big trawlers and seiners of other countries were cruising close to their shore, getting all the big fish and destroying the little ones.

Then someone discovered that South Harbour was alive with oysters! The fishermen staked their claims and oyster fishing was profitable – until the oyster beds were fished out.

Then queen crab was discovered and the fishermen went after that – until there didn't seem to be any more.

In 1976, with the proclamation of a two-hundred-mile limit for foreign vessels, inshore fishing provided a living again.

And swordfish – still basking off Cape Breton's shores – though not saleable in Canada are welcomed in the U.S.A. The fishermen of Neil's Harbour will tell you, "We don't roightly go after 'em but if we sees one out there we'll catch 'en, if we's lucky."

How to Live Without Wars and Wedding Rings

One day in 1949 when I was calling on Bill (W.O.) Mitchell – then fiction editor of *Maclean's* magazine – he introduced me to Pierre Berton, the new articles editor. Bill said, "Edna's swordfishing piece was number one in the readership test; why don't we get her to write a piece for us about the horse-and-buggy Mennonites? She lives in the area."

They discussed the idea and agreed that I should try it.

But what did I really know about the Old Order Mennonites? I saw them in their black bonnets and shawls every Saturday morning at the Kitchener market, selling *kochkase* and vegetables. I heard stories about their strange ways and expressions. How could I find out anything more? "They won't tell you anything," I was told whenever I enquired about them. "They keep to themselves."

I decided the only way was to try to find a family that would let me live with them for a while. At the general store in St. Jacobs I was given the name of a family that was friendly and less withdrawn than most of the Old Order. I approached their farmhouse with some trepidation. A neat little woman wearing a prayer cap invited me into her kitchen. She and her daughter listened to me and shyly agreed that it might not be bad to have their way of life explained so people could understand why they live without cars and radios, telephones, pianos, and pensions.

The woman went out to the barn to discuss my proposal with her husband. She came back smiling, and it was arranged that I'd come to stay with them the following Monday.

N ot long ago I stayed for a week with the family of Gross-doddy Martin, in the fieldstone house his great-grand-father built in the days when the Mennonites came up from Pennsylvania to break new ground in Upper Canada. The house and the family are among the oldest in Ontario – almost two hundred years have passed fruitfully and peacefully over the farm their pioneer forefathers cleared from the wilderness in Waterloo County.

The Martins belong to a splinter sect, the Old Order Men-nonites, whose ways often seem strange to outsiders. They shun everything worldly, everything fashionable, but they don't mind a swig of cider. They use electricity and tractors, but will not buy cars or radios. They won't face a camera. They don't have telephones in their homes, or musical instru-ments. They refuse old-age pensions, medicare, and family allowances. They won't buy insurance or stocks. They won't go to court or to war and Canadian law has been amended to exempt them permanently from both. They speak Pennsyl-vania Dutch and have a look of contentment.

The style of their plain, sombre clothes has changed little since 1525. The men wear broad-brimmed black hats with round crowns; their coats, with old-fashioned cut-away backs, are buttoned straight up the front to a neckband, having no collars or lapels. Their faces are clean-shaven – moustaches, being ornamental, are not allowed. The hair of some men and boys is conventionally cut; others look as if a bowl had been placed over the head and the rim used as a cutting guide.

The women's dark print dresses, made from a traditional pattern, have fitted waists under a pointed plastron, and long, gathered skirts that almost hide their black stockings. Their uncut, uncurled hair is always covered by a white organdie cap tied under the chin, or a helmetlike black satin bonnet. In cold weather they are bundled in shawls. They wear no cosmetics or jewellery – not even wedding rings.

The Old Order Mennonites try to preserve the ways of their forefathers who crossed the Atlantic nearly three hundred years ago to escape religious persecution in Switzerland and settled first in Pennsylvania, then, in 1786, started coming to Canada. Although there are more than 160,000 Mennonites of various sects all the way from Ontario to British Columbia, there are only about 2,500 members of the Old Order. They cling to their homesteads near Waterloo and Kitchener, and their eight similar white-clapboard churches are on their own farmlands, all within a twenty-mile radius.

Like most Old Mennonite farm homes, Grossdoddy Martin's house sprawls. The main house, Georgian Colonial in style, is broad with a gabled roof; the plastered wall under the porch is painted sky blue. Adjoining is the *doddy* (grandfather) house, a small addition to which the generations of old folks have retired when their youngest sons took over the farm. Behind the kitchen is the frame summer kitchen; beyond it the wash-house, the woodshed, and the privy.

Prosperity smiles on the Martin house from its great painted barn. Beauty surrounds it: gentle hills form its horizons, its fields slope to the maple woods along the curving Conestoga River. On the day I arrived, fruit trees beside the house were snowy with blossom and daffodils bordered the neatly fenced lawn.

"You don't want to make fun of us?" The Martins were anxious when I asked if I might live with them for a few days to learn and write about them – though trustful, they were alert. From the beginning they used my Christian name; they were friendly, natural, and disarmingly candid. They answered my questions thoughtfully, generously, and asked me as many in return – only Grossdoddy, listening with a quiet smile, took no part.

I wanted them to speak in their dialect, an unwritten mixture of Swiss-German and English, but they didn't think it would be polite since I couldn't understand all the words. They asked me to correct their English. "We're shy to talk English in front of strangers because we don't say our letters always right: like for Jesus we say 'Cheesus.' We know it's wrong but we forget. Amongst ourselfs we always talk our own kind of German – it's easier; and if we don't, our own people think we're putting on style."

In their house there was little that was not useful except, in the spare room, two bouquets of paper roses that the parents had given the daughters for Christmas, and scenic calendars that had long outlived their dates. All the walls were whitewashed; the woodwork was painted bright blue. The windows had no curtains, but tins of geraniums bloomed on the sills. There were five bedrooms with pumpkin-yellow floors. The tiny parlour had a huge corner cupboard and wooden chairs set side by side against the pictureless walls. The kitchen was also the living-dining-room; the big black stove was always warm, and there was comfort in the couch and the rocker in the corner.

"Make the light on once," Bevvy, the mother, directed after supper on the day I arrived, and the family gathered round the long, oilcloth-covered table. David, the father, worked on his income-tax papers; Salome, sixteen, was absorbed by a romantic novel written fifty years ago; Amsey, seven, and Lyddy Ann, twelve, smiled at me over their schoolbooks; Bevvy placidly turned the pages of the *Family Herald*; Grossdoddy sat in the shadows near the passage to the *doddy* house.

"I was glad to quit school and earn money when I was eleven but often now I wish I went longer yet." David frowned at his papers. "If a person went to college his mind would mature in more of a hurry, I guess."

"The teacher wanted Salome to go longer," Bevvy told me. "She finished school already when she was thirteen, but Mannassah Brubacher's wife needed help chust then, so she went there to work. People hate us for our different ways and if she was in town she would have to act like a turtle for shame or change her Old Mennonite clothes; then she couldn't belong to us no more."

Salome looked up. "I'd like to learn but I wouldn't want to stay from home," she said. "In the city it seems each day is chust like any other day but in the country every day gives something different."

"You can always learn from things you read and people you meet." David's eyes were teasing as they glanced my way. "You think you're going to find out all about us while you're here, but we'll get chust as much from you."

At nine-thirty Bevvy led me up an enclosed stair and through a bare corridor to the spare room where I slept surprisingly well on an ancient rope bed with a straw tick and bolster.

Always the first up in the morning, Grossdoddy put on his stay-at-home suit over the long underwear in which he slept –

I was told – and went into the parlour of the *doddy* house where Grossmommy, a black kerchief on her head, lay sleeping on a hospital bed. A young man rose stiffly from a couch.

"She made nothing out all night," he said, putting on his hat. "I see you next week again." He shook the old man's hand, then went out to harness his horse.

He was one of the relatives or neighbours who, in the kindly custom of the Old Order, took turns to come every night from nine o'clock till dawn to relieve the Martin family of some of the care of Grossmommy's lingering illness.

"We always look after our own," Bevvy told me. "And if we don't have enough money for doctors it's paid from the church."

"Why don't you take government benefits?"

"If we did we wouldn't feel independent," she said. "You know we got promised religious freedom a long time ago and that our men don't have to fight in a war."

"Would they if our own country was attacked?" I asked.

Bevvy thoughtfully shook her head. "Jesus said we must turn the other cheek; if everyone did that there would be no wars."

"But everyone in the world doesn't practise Jesus' teaching."

"Then we must be an example." Bevvy smiled. "In the last war our boys helped with the wounded and went in work camps and we bought war bonds." She added hastily, "But we didn't take the interest off them; that would be profiting from war."

When the morning milking was finished, Salome, singing "Throw out the Lifeline" in her clear, young voice, drew the full cans to the cooler in a little cart. Topsy, the collie, followed her.

The hens and beeplings fed, Lyddy Ann pointed out a red patch by the river. "Amsey went fishing at five already. Can you see him down there near the willow?"

At the kitchen sink David pumped rainwater into the basin to wash his face and arms. Bevvy, by the range, ran plump fingers through the curds that would be made into *kochkase* (cook cheese).

"Make the door shut, Salome. We won't wait for Amsey."

David was hungry: he had been doing barn chores for almost two hours.

Bevvy tucked a wisp of hair under the grey kerchief that had covered her head during the night. "I'll comb myself after breakfast," she said.

Chairs were drawn up to the table, heads bowed silently over ironstone plates. Grossdoddy reached for coffee cake with his fork. Everyone stabbed a piece and dunked it. Amsey came in, pleased with ten pink-headed chub. Porridge was eaten, the remains sopped up with bread so the plates could be filled with fried potatoes, summer sausage, and pickled beans. A bowl of *schnitz und gwetcha* (boiled dried apple segments and prunes) was passed.

There was talk of the day's work to be done, of things growing; there were questions and answers, and there was laughter.

"Dat, you said slang," little Amsey chided his big Mennonite father with the warm brown eyes.

"Did I? Now what bad word did I say?" David pretended alarm.

"You said 'swell.'" The child was very serious.

"Och, ain't that awful? I must be more careful or my children won't be brought up decent," David declared. "But ain't 'swell' a bad word that could be used good?"

When we rose the plates looked as clean as when we sat down. Though it was only seven-thirty, Amsey and Lyddy Ann, eager to play with other children, ran across the fields to school. David went to plough with the tractor. Grossdoddy sat with Grossmommy; Salome sang as she washed the breakfast dishes.

At the little mirror above the kitchen sink Bevvy combed her hair, which fell below her waist. "We never cut them," she told me, "and we all do them chust about the same."

Parting her hair in the centre, she wet it to straighten its curl, folded it flat at the sides like the wings of a bird and then wound it into a spiral pinned firmly on the back of her head. As she tied a dainty white organdie bonnet with black ribbons under her chin, she said, "It's in the Bible that women should keep their heads covered when they pray and we might pray any time of the day or night." Bevvy never sounds pious: she accepts her rules as she does the planting of seed and the harvest.

Salome, looking through the window above the sink, exclaimed, "Isn't that pear tree beautiful? I often thought already I'd like to be able to draw it."

"May you draw pictures?" I asked.

"I may but I couldn't," she said.

"We chust mayn't have pictures on our walls or make pictures of ourselfs," Bevvy explained. "It is in the Ten Commandments, you know, about not making a likeness. Our retired bishop is real old and his children in Pennsylvania want him in the worst way to spend the rest of his days with them but he can't because he would have to have his picture taken for a passport and that would set a bad example."

Among the Old Mennonites example is a powerful force, I learned from the Martins. Young people emulate those who are older; the preachers urge adherence to the ways of their ancestors. If these humble people are permitted any pride, it is in their traditions. Their forefathers braved perils and hardships for their faith, clung to their beliefs, and died for them.

The Mennonite creed arose when the establishment of a state church in Switzerland was opposed, in 1525, by a group of former monks and scholars who wanted a religious order that was free of compulsion. The new sect spread rapidly over north Switzerland; it taught only love, faith, forbearance, and adult baptism, but its followers were exiled, tortured, or burned at the stake. Believing that evil would be overcome by goodness, they would not defend themselves against attack, and thousands of martyrs died without offering resistance.

In 1538 Menno Simons, a former Roman Catholic priest who had become a convert, reorganized and consolidated their congregations, which became known by his name. Services were held secretly in houses and barns; when educated leaders were imprisoned or murdered, simple farmers chosen by lot became preachers and bishops. The humble Mennonites, evicted from one place, would patiently begin again in another till they ranged throughout central Europe. Wherever they settled the land blossomed under their care.

Persecution continued for more than two hundred years.

From 1683 on, thousands of Mennonites accepted the invitation of William Penn, whose Quaker faith was similar to theirs, to come to America where Britain promised them freedom from military service and the right to worship as they pleased.

Because they wanted to keep the security of British citizenship after the American Revolution, and because land was less expensive in Upper Canada than in Pennsylvania, hundreds of Mennonites brought their families in Conestoga wagons on the seven-week journey across swamps, mountains, and the terrifying Niagara. Some stayed near the Canadian frontier but most pushed on to Waterloo County, where they became the first white settlers in the interior of the province.

"And from them came all the different kinds of Mennonites around here," David told me.

"Except the Mennonites that came over from Russia," Bevvy corrected.

"Yah, that's right. We don't know much about any but our own. The others mostly all have churches in the towns and they don't dress or act like us Old Mennonites." In this way David dismissed the majority of Mennonite sects.

The first break from the pioneer church in Waterloo County was made in 1869 when a group was ceremoniously evicted because it wanted evangelism. The desire for English services, camp meetings, Sunday schools, young-people's societies, higher education, and the free use of invention and of modern but modest dress resulted in further divisions. Quite separate from but similar to the pioneers were the 15,000 Mennonites who came from Russia in 1874 and settled in Manitoba and Saskatchewan, and the thousands who were forced from their homes by the Bolsheviks in the 1920s and found refuge in Ontario and western Canada.

"In Kitchener there is a Mennonite high school and in Waterloo and Preston an old-people's home; there's Conrad Greble College at Waterloo University," Bevvy told me. "And they have a Mennonite central committee where all the kinds of Mennonites go together and sew and send food and clothes and implements to Mennonites in other parts of the world to give to people in need, no matter who they are. I think that's real nice but our old folks don't want us to work in town so we have sewing bees in our own homes and send the committee what we make." Because it might seem boastful, Bevvy went on reluctantly, "We give them food and money too, but we mostly just care for our neighbours and our own; like if a man's barn burns down we build him a new one, if his cows die we give him some, or we help with his work if he's sick. That's the Golden Rule," she said simply.

"Why aren't there more Old Order Mennonites?" I asked. Bevvy blushed. "In Canada there's only us around here."

"There's some in Pennsylvania and Ohio," David said, "only they're a little different from us yet, but we visit back and forth and are related with each other."

"We can marry back and forth too," Bevvy added, "but it's chenerally only the leftovers that do; most Old Mennonites get partners at home where their parents can buy them a farm."

"We like to stay all together like," David explained. "It makes it easier for us to keep our rules if we aren't mixed up with other people."

"Do you think the rest of us are so bad?" I asked.

"Ach no." Bevvy was embarrassed. "We think there's good and bad the same as with us, we chust have different ways."

"Like the Newborns," David said, "they broke off from us because they thought we were going too fast by having the electric and tractors; they wanted to be more backward yet. And the Markham Mennonites wanted cars and telephones so they got out, but they still use our churches every other Sunday and they paint their cars black with no chrome and dress about the same as we do."

One day the roadside post box had a packet in it for Salome. "It's the books we sent for with the boxtops." She opened it excitedly. One book was a novel, the other a collection of old songs from which she started singing "My Darling Nellie Gray." If I had told her that her voice is beautiful she would have blushed. She had no ambition or vain thought of performing on radio, television, or in Hollywood, though she has eagerness, imagination, wit, a gay red mouth, merry eyes, and the roundest of elbows. When a strand of her soft brown hair escapes its severity her mother reproves her, but Salome laughingly says, "It looks nicest when it's *shtruvelich* [tousled]."

"Here comes Uncle Isaiah." Lyddy Ann had started reading

Salome's novel the moment she came home from school but she reported every movement on the road. An old man with a strong, stern face came into the kitchen and shook hands all around.

"How is Auntie Katie?" Bevvy asked him.

"She ain't goot. She's got the high blood pressure yet and the doctor says she must lose some fat but she can't – it's natural. Her mother and father together weighed near five hundred pounds." The old man shook his head despairingly, then settled in a corner to chat with Grossdoddy.

While we peeled potatoes for supper Bevvy said to me, "You haf such a nice apron."

"I'll let you have the pattern for it."

She grinned. "No thanks, we couldn't have one so fancy. Our clothes are supposed to be all alike and plain so we won't think about how we look. They protect us from temptation too; we couldn't go to picture shows or places of entertainment without being noticed."

"Leave me show her how we dress in winter." Salome ran upstairs; in a few minutes she was back, shaped like an enormous black beehive. Only her delicate nose and sparkling eyes revealed the lovely girl.

"Salome, I wouldn't know you if we met on the street," I exclaimed.

"You would." She laughed. "I'd yell at you."

A wool crêpe veil was folded over her forehead and pinned around the satin bonnet; a thick, fringed shawl fastened with a blanket pin covered a loose black coat, and a smaller shawl muffled her chin.

"It's cold in an open cutter," she explained as she took off the layers of clothes. "See, I fold my shawl straight – if I was married I'd have a point down the back." She handed me her black satin bonnet: it was stiff and heavy as a steel helmet and a little bit faded. "That I had since I finished school already."

"She'll have to take good care of it till she's twenty-one, then we'll buy her a whole new outfit and have her bonnet made over," Bevvy told me while Salome returned her things to the closet.

"Is that when she'll be married?"

"Not necessary, but she might be if she's found a partner she likes. Every Sunday evening the young folks go together to someone's house for a 'singing'; they learn our hymns that way and play games and Salome says some of them dance – but they're not supposed to. If a boy and girl like each other he might drive her home in his buggy."

I faltered over my next question: "Do they bundle?"

"Bundle? What's that?" Bevvy's innocence was honest; I couldn't pursue the subject.

"Does she go out with different boys?" I asked.

"Och, no, she sticks to the one she chooses at the beginning, usually. She could fire him at the end of a year or two and go with another but never more than two or she'd have a bad name and for the boys it's the same – no girl would want to go with a boy that would run from one to another. It's not like in the city where young people go out with strangers; we know the parents and grandparents of everybody from way back and we can pretty well tell if a marriage will be all right. We mayn't have divorces. Only one Old Mennonite married man we know ever went with another woman, and of course now he's out of the church."

After supper the children were in a gay mood. They cleaned the fish Amsey had caught after school; they patted the cats. Lyddy Ann picked violets; Salome played her mouth organ (the only musical instrument allowed). They pranced around the pansy bed; Lyddy Ann held sticks for Topsy to jump at; Salome sang a song. We smelled the honeysuckle and the daffodils; when darkness came we looked at the stars.

"I often wondered already how the streetlights look when they're on in Kitchener and Waterloo," Salome said wistfully.

"Do you never go to town?" I asked. The cities were only eight miles away.

"Oh yes, to the dentist."

"But we have always to be home in time for the milking," Lyddy Ann lamented.

Amsey was looking at the north star. "I would like once to see a ship," he declared.

"I too," said Lyddy Ann. "I would like to travel round the world."

"I would go with you," the little boy said, "and if we came to some cannibals they would eat me last because I am the skinniest."

At nine o'clock Bevvy called, "Come in now, children, and wash your feet before you go in bed."

On Sunday morning Grossdoddy drove Salome and me to church; he sat on one of each of our knees while we sat on the narrow seat of his buggy.

Martin's Meeting House, on the highway north of Waterloo, is more than a hundred years old; its painted clapboards gleam white. A wire fence surrounds its yard, kept neat by a munching cow, and the cemetery beside it where rows and rows of plain white slabs mark the grassy, flowerless graves. There are no family plots: here Nathanial Lichty, Josiah Ernst, Susannah Eby, Israel Weber, Veronica Erb, Rebecca Shantz – and the stillborn infants of David and Bevvy Martin – lie side by side.

Open buggies, two-seaters and boxlike *dachwaegles* (top buggies) came in a steady stream as the black-clad people gathered to worship. Horses pranced up to the cement stoop along one side of the building. Women and little girls in shawls and bonnets alighted; grandmothers went through a door near the front, mothers and children near the centre, young girls hurried to the back. Men and boys drove to the hitching chains, then entered the church on the farther end. In a crowded cloakroom on the women's side, shawls hung on wooden pegs and black bonnets lay on shelves; on the heads of the rosy-cheeked, chattering girls were caps of white organdie with pale coloured ribbons tied under their chins. The style of their hair and their print cotton dresses had no variation.

Light flooded the church from small-paned windows, walls were whitewashed, scrubbed pine floors and benches were worn smooth and shiny. Women sat on one side, men on the other, on benches that were half the length of the church, each bench a step higher than the one in front of it. In the aisle between them were two stoves with long smokestacks. Suspended from the ceiling above each bench on the men's side were wooden bars with wooden pegs for the men's broad-brimmed hats.

A long, desklike lectern in the centre front of the church had an open space before it to be used for baptism and feet-washing ceremonies. Behind the lectern five men sat side by side; a sixth man approached, kissed and shook hands with the others, then took his place among them.

"That's our preacher," Salome whispered to me. "The others are preachers too and our bishop."

Chosen for life by lot from slips of paper drawn from a Bible, the Old Order Mennonite preacher, Salome told me, is also a farmer. He receives no pay, prepares no written sermons: his spontaneous word is believed to be inspired. And he has authority. If a church member buys what he is not supposed to, marries outside the Old Order, gets drunk too often, or does worldly things, the preacher will speak to him privately. If the vanity or sin is not repented, if it is irremissible, the erring one is denounced before the congregation. Though cast out of the church, he is not treated unkindly and, if contrite, may return.

Salome opened a hymn book printed in German script. Led by a man's voice, the congregation sat while it droned each syllable; the bishop preached for half an hour. The members of the congregation, turning to face their seats, knelt for silent prayer, their backs to the front of the church. "To live honestly and at peace with all men" was the text of the preacher's hour-long sermon in Pennsylvania Dutch.

Throughout the service the older men and women sat very still but in the long benches in front there was constant movement of babies and tiny children being hushed or taken to the cloakroom by mothers with bulging satchels. Two rows of lively little girls, their braids tied with string or a bit of shoe-lace, couldn't restrain a few giggles. The young girls who sat high at the back of the church turned solemn eyes towards the preacher or stole glances at the young men on the high benches at the other side of the room.

During the last hymn the little ones filed into the cloak-room. Babies in bright print or lustre dresses, black stockings and colorful bootees were bundled up in black or purple shawls. The service over, women and children clustered on the cement stoop to chat till their men drove up smartly to pick them up in their buggies or two-seated wagons.

Salome blushingly told me she was invited out for the day.

"Sunday is our visiting day," Bevvy explained. "Sometimes we have twenty people drop in for a meal."

"And don't you know they're coming?" I asked.

"Not always, they chust come after church. When Menno Horsts moved to the farm over there behind those maples they had fifty-six the first Sunday." She smiled. "Everyone was inquisitif to see their new house."

"How do you feed them?"

"Ach, that don't bother us, everybody helps. There's always lots in the cellar or the garden, and every Friday we bake cakes and buns and nine or ten pies. If somebody comes they're all eaten at one time and if not we haf them the rest of the week."

During the next three days the Martins answered many more of my questions.

"The preachers tell us to vote if we need a new bridge or something like that, but we don't know enough about politics to vote for the country. Artificial insemination of our cattle gives us better stock. With electricity we can do more work. Salome can run the tractor. Telephones we may have in the barn for business – if we sell fresh meat or the like of that – but not in our houses for pleasure.

"We wouldn't want our children to hear some of the things on the radio or television. If we had musical instruments we mightn't sing so much ourselfs. We never heard yet of any of our people stealing or getting in any trouble with the law."

I told them a story I'd heard about a man who tried to sell a car to an Old Mennonite. The farmer said he couldn't buy it because the devil was in it.

"But what about the gasoline motor you use?" the salesman asked. "It's the same thing – isn't the devil in that too?"

"Maybe, but he's fastened down and I can make him do whatever I want, in a car he's running around and might get out of control."

The family laughed heartily. "That sounds chust like something old Levi Gingerich would say," David said. "He'd have an answer for anybody that tried to get smart with him."

"We take a ride in a car sometimes but it would be a danger and a temptation for our young people to own one," Bevvy explained. "Anyways we love to ride behind our horses – they go fast enough for us.

"Some things we do to stay different and separate: it makes it easier to keep our rules. We don't know why we have some of them. They were handed to us from generation to generation; they're not written down. The bishop and the preachers have to change them sometimes or make new ones, but if we don't like what they tell us we can put them out of the church and do what we think is right.

"We don't believe in converting people to our ways; we leave them alone and want to be left alone – religion should be quiet and deep in the heart, not on the tongue. We're supposed to live simple so we can have more time to think about the Lord; if we got stylish we might get proud. We could never be clever like other people anyway – we're chust farmers, we love best to watch things grow, and work makes us happy."

"We like being boss on our own land," David said with an air of unallowed pride. "I would hate to have to work for somebody else that would tell me what I should or shouldn't do."

On the last night of my stay in the fieldstone house, the family sat with me on the porch waiting for the car that would come to take me away. I said, "I haven't heard a cross or grumbling word since I came here. Don't you ever get mad? Don't your children ever quarrel or disobey? Are you never tired of working? Do you never break your rules?"

They looked at one another and laughed. "We've all been extra good this week because you were here," Lyddy Ann said.

"We were telling you what all we're supposed to do but we don't always do it." Bevvy grinned.

Salome brought me a hyacinth, Grossdoddy gave me a willow whistle he'd made, Topsy pushed against my hand for a pat, there was the scent of honeysuckle and blossoms, the sound of frogs near the river.

Salome said to me, "You are so quiet now, why don't you talk?"

"I was thinking how peaceful it is here," I said.

David nodded. "That's what I often think."

"In the world I'm going back to we are always fighting for peace."

Maclean's, April 1, 1950

☆　☆　☆　☆　☆

Throughout the many years since I went to live with the Martins we have become good friends and spent much enjoyable time together. Though their rules and beliefs and lifestyle are the same as they've always been, there have been other changes in their lives.

Bevvy and David now drive to church in a *dachwaegle* and sit on the front benches with the old folks. They no longer live in their ancestral stone farmhouse – David's well-tilled fields will inevitably become a housing development. They are comfortable in a neat little house in the country beside the large, modern home of their son Amsey, who has ten children and drives a big black car with no chrome to his very successful business in town.

Salome and Lyddy Ann live on farms of their own with their husbands; their younger children attend Old Order parochial schools, and their older ones are thinking of being married.

"But the land where our people always lived is too near the cities and costs too much for our young people. When they buy farms now they have to go so far away that we'll not have much time with our great-grandchildren," Bevvy laments. "Quite a few now are living around Mount Forest, they've got two churches there already, but it's fifty miles away and that's too far for us to drive with a horse."

"Ach yes, but we'll get there," David says. "We can hire a car. And you'll see our young people will get along; they'll get along the same as we always did."

The Isles of Codfish and Champagne

*I*n September 1949, my flight to Sydney, Nova
Scotia (en route to a Neil's Harbour vacation), was
delayed in Halifax by stormy weather. As usual when
I'm in Halifax, I haunted the waterfront where I was
intrigued by a tubby little freighter called *Miquelon*.
I soon found out she belonged to the French islands
of Saint Pierre and Miquelon and that, if I wanted to,
I could be a passenger and visit the islands, just three
hundred fifty miles away. I'd go to Neil's Harbour on
my return.

I asked many questions about Saint Pierre but no
one I met in Halifax had been there, though everyone
warned me I'd better be cautious: "You know how
Frenchmen go for wine and women." Also I was told
to board the *Miquelon* at North Sydney to shorten
the trip by one hundred fifty miles "because she rolls
something awful in weather."

S aint Pierre, the merry little port that was a reservoir of liquor in the days of American prohibition, lies just twelve miles from Newfoundland's Burin Peninsula and seventy minutes by air from Sydney, Nova Scotia. It is the capital of the Territory of the Isles of Saint Pierre and Miquelon, the oldest and smallest possession of France. The tiny metropolis clings to the motherland and governs its colony of 4,800 people with ten gendarmes sent over from France and three hundred civil servants.

There are no bootlegging boats in the harbour now; the smell of cod is stronger than that of rum, and empty liquor warehouses on 11th of November Street are used for prize fights and French movies. In the cafés fishermen drink champagne, on the waterfront straw-stuffed sabots clatter, and Chanel No. 5 is displayed in a hundred shop windows with leeks, Benedictine, and dainties from Paris.

It was fish that brought the French to the islands in the fourteenth century. While France and Britain fought to possess the New World, the British captured and burned Saint Pierre three times before the Treaty of Paris, in 1814, finally allowed France to keep the islands as a fishing base. Nestling under Newfoundland like eggs under a hen, the archipelago, with its four villages and one town, its ninety-three square miles of hills and bogs, its reefs and rocky coasts dimmed by fog or hidden by winter snow, is all that France has left of her vast North American empire.

The largest and most northerly island is Miquelon, with five hundred people in one melancholy village that has no harbour. Joined to it by a seven-mile sandbar is beautiful green Langlade, with a few summer homes, two farms, and a stony beach. Saint Pierre Island, though smaller, boasts the capital, two fishing settlements, half a dozen farms, about eighteen miles of road, and a harbour facing France. Roughly rectangular in shape, with a bulge on the east side where all the people live, it is about five miles long and less than half as wide. Most of it is volcanic rock. It has no trees; if a sapling appears it is cut down for firewood or a fence. Scraggly bushes try to cover its mountains (so-called), but they give up near the summits, which are bald and grey, presenting a thrilling view of more hills, clear pools, deep bays, the dim coast of Newfoundland, and the huddling little port.

44

Not many travellers find their way to Saint Pierre – which is one of its charms – and those who do can never be sure how or when they can leave it. Maritime Central Airways sends a twenty-one-passenger plane up from Sydney every week if there is no fog, no rain, no wind. The *Blue Seal*, a freighter with accommodation for ten, calls monthly en route from Montreal to St. John's, but does not stop on the return trip. The most reliable way of getting off the island is on the *Miquelon*, the rolling little steamer that belongs to the French government. M. Morazé, her manager in Saint Pierre, can predict her departure almost to the day. Of course, emergencies arise: the soccer team may want transportation to Newfoundland; it may be necessary to run over to Langlade to fetch someone home for a funeral; sometimes the *Miquelon* takes a trip to France. Usually she runs to and from Halifax or Sydney three times a month; anyone who happens to be where she is can get a ride for around fifty dollars.

I flew to Sydney to be one of seven passengers on the crowded little vessel. It took eighteen hours to reach Saint Pierre. My shipmate was a flirtatious matron with an English vocabulary of three words: "okay," "thanks," and "water closet." M. and Mme Dagort, returning from an annual visit with their daughter in France, shared their tiny cabin with a young man who, like all well-to-do Saint Pierrais, had spent a year learning English in Canada. "Saint Pierre is just like one family," they told me. Mme Flahaut had with her an eleven-year-old niece from Montreal whose lively *canadien* manners and slangy patois embarrassed the ladies of Saint Pierre. "We cannot interpret her French; it is of Jacques Cartier's time, not *moderne* as in Saint Pierre and in Paris," they explained.

They all addressed me in English but spoke to each other in French, which I could not understand; we smiled at each other and felt very friendly.

They told me that everyone loves the town of Saint Pierre. On its lonely little island in a cold and foggy sea, it is a welcome haven where the crews of French trawlers unload their fish and find a bit of comfort, where schooners from Canada's coast come in for untaxed liquor, cigarettes, and "a time." It is a town of four thousand people, very well-behaved. The young man sharing the Dagorts' cabin told me, "In every house a woman sits behind the lace curtains watching everyone that pass. If I take out two, three different girls I am bad boy; if I take always one to dance I am expect to marry wis her." He added that Saint Pierre's feeble electricity, which comes on at dusk, fades out gently at midnight. "Except in the cafés." Mme Flahaut rolled her eyes. "There everybody dance, everybody drink champagne."

On the *Miquelon*, M. Dagort ordered a round of grapefruit juice; we watched the sunset, then retired to our cabins.

Next morning everyone on the *Miquelon* peered anxiously into a fog. The engines stopped. "Always this happen when we come near our little country," they told me. The engines started, stopped, started; the foghorn blared.

At lunch the steward announced, "We arrive." I ran to the bow. Saint Pierre was before me, strange and enchanting; it belonged to the Old World, not to America at all. A ridge rising high above the sea crowded the town round the harbour where the ships pointed to the Quai de la Roncière, a broad, open space – partly macadamized – with a fountain that didn't play, and a roofless little bandstand on an oblong of tufted grass in the centre of it, faded, flat-faced buildings round the three land sides, like the backdrop for a stage set long ago and far away.

As we approached, Saint Pierrais rushed over the quay to the wharf till it was crowded with people and dogs eagerly watching. The berets on the men came from France, I was told; the clothes on the women from Eaton's and Simpsons, ordered by mail from Montreal. The blue eyes and blonde hair came from Brittany perhaps four hundred fifty years ago with the first settlers, the dark, handsome faces from the Basque country, the sparkling black eyes from Normandy.

The solemn-faced pair standing aloof in high pill-box hats and khaki uniforms were gendarmes waiting to conduct me – a foreigner from Canada – to customs, where I became wealthy by exchanging a few trim dollars for handfuls of tattered franc notes too limp and too large for my wallet. (The day's legal rate of exchange in Saint Pierre was one hundred francs for sixty-three cents – double the rate in France.)

Bystanders offered to carry my bags across the quay to the wooden Hotel Robert with its fourteen rooms and several baths at 450 francs a day with meals and *vin ordinaire*. Preferring a place less expensive, I rode in a truck to the restaurant-home of Mme Dutin, which had been recommended to me by a man on the quay.

Madame's daughter, Marianne, petite, seventeen, and lovely, was laughingly kissed by my driver, who refused my tip and ordered a round of liqueurs. "Me good Saint Pierre boy," he said, "me wery correct wis you for learn English. Will you go dance wis me tonight?"

Mme Dutin, stout, sharp-eyed, and generous, had been a Newfoundlander. Many of the working people of Saint Pierre, she told me, have Newfoundland mothers. Because finding maids was always a problem, Frenchmen sometimes went to the outports and brought back fishermen's daughters who were eager to work in the fabled gay world of Saint Pierre. They were taught to speak French, they enjoyed French wine, and they learned to make crêpes Suzettes, leek soup, *patisserie*, and potatoes fried crisp and golden in olive oil. They married men of Saint Pierre. Finding maids is still a problem.

After tea and hot raisin buns Marianne invited me to walk with her on the quay. The quay is the heart of Saint Pierre. Life flows to and from the vessels at the piers, to and from the cafés, the shops, the fish company offices, the butter-coloured post office with the bonnetlike roof on its tower. The quay is crossed by everyone who goes to the fine white church and yellow government buildings just around the corner. Salt-scarred trucks rattle over it. Blue and silver *bicyclettes* flash across it. Little crowds gather round the workmen on the wharves.

We saw a child get a basin of fish heads from a man in a dory. A priest zoomed down the hill on a bike, wearing a beret, a beard, a long-skirted robe, and a cape that flowed behind him like wings. There were dozens of dogs: poodles, Newfoundlands, hounds and mongrels that were odd combinations. Young mothers walked two abreast with very new perambulators and babies covered with pink satin. Men in rubber boots or sabots lounged against café walls; crusty golden loaves of bread bounced in a dogcart led by a little girl with blue hair-bows.

We heard rapid French conversation on the windy square; the bleat of a Renault sedan; the roar of a gasoline engine; the noise of hammers. We heard sleigh bells – yes, sleigh bells –

jingling in summer as a milkman's horse drew a two-wheeled cart carrying cases of milk frothing in champagne bottles.

At the nearest pier the *Miquelon* was unloading coal. Beyond her the rusty old *Fuydroyant* had been pouring out salt for a week. She was the victim of the last piracy on the Atlantic. In the days of prohibition she used to come over from France to sell liquor to boats that crept out from the U.S. coast. One night she was boarded by gangsters who held her officers captive till they sold off her cargo themselves.

Marianne spoke proudly of the *Joseph du Hamel*, top trawler on the Banks and winner of the Croix de Guerre for gallantry during the war. Her brother is one of the sixty-six men aboard. In a week they'd be fishing again before going to France for the winter.

The *Téméraire* was waiting to come in. The *Capitaine Armand's* men were on strike: they were tired, dirty, and lonely, had worked hard at the fishing for three or four months, and they wanted to go home to France. They lounged in Saint Pierre's cafés.

The tubby little *Béarn*, half Saint Pierre's navy, had just come in from Langlade where she goes every Tuesday in summer and during the September partridge shooting; on Friday she delivers supplies to the island of Miquelon.

A Canadian freighter was going out; she'd brought vegetables, chickens, and calves. Seven rowboats had come from Newfoundland with sheep tied to their gunwales. Four high-masted schooners were in for the night and the harbour was swarming with dories. A seaplane took off from the roadstead.

Everyone in Saint Pierre seemed to be on the quay. It is fashionable to come there to learn what is going on. No newspapers reach the island; radio reception is rare; telephones are installed in business establishments only. But mail comes in almost every week, Western Union transatlantic cables are relayed at Saint Pierre, a blackboard in front of Henry Morazé's announces events to come, and of course anyone you meet might give you a morsel of gossip.

"They've not yet found Mlle de Gasse who prayed at a hillside shrine and wandered away on a foggy morning last week," we were told.

"Yves and Gabrielle are betrothed." We hurried home to tell Marianne's *maman*.

Waiting for me in the Dutins' kitchen was a dapper gendarme who had come to collect a fine of 800 francs (five dollars) because I'd entered the country without a passport. Mme Dutin poured him an aperitif. He settled down to tell us how bored he is in such a good town as Saint Pierre. The guillotine is never needed; perhaps once a year there is a theft; only occasionally a rum-fired sailor is taken to the *gendarmerie* with the broken bottles sticking out of its walls. "Ees mostly stranger drink in Saint Pierre too much." He sipped his thimble of wine. "Saint Pierrais have only a leetle bit often: to make pleasure with a *camarade*, at a meal *c'est nécessaire* for *de digestion*, a liqueur in the coffee ees very nice and brandee before bed, onless there ees veesitor, or dancing, den opens POP! ze champagne."

"One time dere was murder in Saint Pierre," Mme Dutin told us. A fisherman killed his dory mate, cut him in pieces, and salted him. The criminal court condemned the man to death. A guillotine was constructed but there was no executioner. No one in Saint Pierre wanted to be one. At last a man was bribed to do the horrible job. The guillotine had never been tested – what if it wouldn't work? They tried it out on a calf. Slick. But when the murderer came to the block his head would not quite sever. It had to be cut off with a knife. No one in Saint Pierre would speak to the executioner after that. He went to live in France.

After dinner, at eight, Marianne took me to a hole-in-the-wall café. Seated at tiny tables were men in ships' officers' uniforms, young sailors wearing berets, Saint Pierre boys in jackets, very black men from Senegal in white shirts. Newfoundland fishermen in heavy, peaked caps looked wistful. "Can only dance the squares or the Kintish Rambles. I'd thank ye, dear, if ye wouldn't moind settin' out," they said to the girls, the laughing pretty girls of Saint Pierre, who could have a hundred partners.

Vivacious Fleurette, with hair dyed red, was busy behind the bar. Marianne ordered juice. Everyone else drank champagne and almost behaved with decorum. A little boy changed records on a loud and ancient machine ("*C'est si bon*," "*Je vous aime beaucoup,"* "Drifting Down the River on a Sunday Afternoon"). We watched the couples swaying on the greasy softwood floor.

"Dansez, mam'selle, s'il vous plait!" With dignity and gaiety Marianne joined the dancers.

"Mama does not me allow to have a boy till I am another year," she said as we ran home before the streetlights faded at midnight.

Next day I wandered around the town. Some streets radiate from the quay; some are parallel to the waterfront, then dwindle away to the hills. They have no sidewalks, no trees, no grassy lawns; 107 shops are scattered among 700 clapboard houses that touch one another flat against narrow gravel roads where cars and trucks with handmade licence plates up to number 151 have to honk at pedestrians and sleeping dogs to get the right-of-way.

There are butcher shops and baker shops and some that specialize in ships' supplies, in hardware, stationery, china; most have a general mixture and some have empty shelves. In dim interiors are rows and rows of bottles with prices marked in francs: apricot brandy 105 francs a quart (about seventy Canadian cents), crème de menthe 134 francs (one dollar), anisette 138 francs, Benedictine 242 francs, Muscat, Malaga, St. Rafael, Napoleon, all 165 francs, Pernot, Dubonnet, Cointreau, cognac, whisky, rum, beer, and champagne for seventy cents a bottle.

Shelves of groceries and clothing have Canadian brand names and prices. Most popular are cartons of delicate wafers, boiled sweets, chocolate, and pickles from France. Handmade French lace is twenty cents a yard. There are dainty kid gloves, Swiss watches for fifteen dollars, pipes, jewellery, cameras for a song, and cosmetics, the very best from Paris, for fifty francs a box. Perfumes that are forty dollars in Montreal – they told me – are four dollars in Saint Pierre.

Dominique Borotra, one-time mayor of Miquelon and member of the governing Counseil General, waited quietly alone in the most modern shop. His deep-set eyes were sad as he looked at half-empty shelves.

"Almost everything we need is bought from Canada," he

told me, "and we have not enough dollars to pay. France makes up the difference for us. But will France forever keep pouring money into Saint Pierre for nothing but codfish?" The old man sighed. "Perhaps because I am old my heart is fearful. It would not be easy to see our country sold; we have preserved here well the French way of life; to us it is most precious. I don't know what will happen to us; we go up and we go down. I am perplexed and very tired."

The flashy red Nash in front of Landry and Co.'s tobacco and wine shop was waiting for genial Georges Landry who, as president of the board of trade – and father-in-law of the governor – was given special permission to import an American car because every day he must drive out to inspect Le Frigo, the great concrete fish-freezing plant that stands on the edge of the roadstead. The decaying building, which cost seventeen million francs, has not been freezing fish for thirty years, yet it represents the colony's only industry: the shipping of fish caught off the shores of the islands and the transshipping of salt cod brought in by the trawlers.

Le Frigo was built after the First World War to store fish for the French trawler fleet but in 1923, when the U.S. was thirsty, Saint Pierre forgot about fish. Le Frigo held a million bottles of Scotch. In most of the houses, spare bedrooms and basements were filled with champagne. The ancient naval barracks stored cognacs and liqueurs; warehouses for rum and Canadian rye were built along the waterfront. A hundred boats waited in the harbour to take on contraband.

The traffic was perfectly legal, of course, from Saint Pierre's point of view. There was nothing wrong with selling liquor to whoever came to fetch it. Boats were dutifully cleared by customs. There was no trouble till they left the islands to hide their treasure in caves, woodsheds, and forests along the mainland coast, dodging the fleet of American and Canadian naval cutters that patrolled the channels to Saint Pierre.

Fortunes were made by the American racketeers who established offices in Saint Pierre and by a few Saint Pierrais who were their agents. A government tax on liquor balanced the budget of the colony, provided a reserve, built roads, wharves, reservoirs for water. Merchants imported fancy goods to sell to visiting smugglers, hotels were filled, cafés overflowed, the private finances of everyone in the colony soared.

In 1933 the United States decided to drink legally again. The bootleggers closed their offices in Saint Pierre. The colony's easy money was gone. Le Frigo was empty. Fishermen mended their nets – but they had forgotten how to live like fishermen. Haunted by the ghost of prosperity, the little town grew shabby. Labourers loafed on the quay.

Then came the Second World War. When the Nazis entered France, Saint Pierre was brokenhearted. She was also in a dilemma. The entire French fishing fleet rushed from the Grand Banks into her little harbour; rusty steam trawlers, cordiers, handliners, barques, and barquentines were jammed in rail to rail. Their crews, fourteen hundred lusty, hungry, unpaid men, swarmed all over the port. Food and wine stocks were depleted; the girls of Saint Pierre were advised to stay at home until, after two months, the fleet made a run for Casablanca.

The governor of the islands arranged for the use of French credits in New York and Montreal to provide his people with food. He tried to keep them submissive to Vichy but the Ancient Combatants, veterans of the First World War, became enthusiastic de Gaullists. There were unarmed battles on the quay. One hundred fifty young men and women escaped to Newfoundland or Canada to join the Free French forces.

Early in the morning of December 23, 1941, four French corvettes came in battle line to Saint Pierre. The sleepy people tumbled down to the quay shouting, *"Vive de Gaulle."* In half an hour, steel-helmeted landing parties carrying tommy guns and flasks of *vin ordinaire* had taken over the town. The Vichy executives were held on the flagship of the little flotilla. Next day a plebiscite was taken and 98 per cent of the colony voted for Free France. The male population was mobilized at last and troops were stationed in the colony till the war was over.

Now the one hundred motor dories of Saint Pierre go out every day the weather permits. "They bring in less fish in a year than one small French trawler will unload after three months on the Banks," M. Landry told me. "But the fishermen, usually the poorest people of any land, can live better here than they could anywhere else in the world. France gives allowances to every child, to all wives who stay home, assists unemployment insurance, subsidizes three schools, gives scholarships for study in France, pays old-age pensions, gives care to mothers and babies, provides an old-people's home and a hospital with two military doctors. All but fifty families own their homes, which have hot running water, electricity, central heating, and always red wine on the table."

In his office M. Landry poured glasses of Benedictine. "Our people complain about weather and boredom, as people do everywhere." He shrugged his well-padded shoulders. "Young people talk about leaving, adventure stirs in their blood, but they won't leave; if they do they'll come back. They know there is no place in the world where they can live so well and work so little. Some talk of belonging to Canada: if we did, our identity would be lost – our cafés, our wines, our way of life. We keep them only if we remain French."

France has a ten-year social and economic plan for her colonies and it is well begun in Saint Pierre. A new school is being erected; an orphans' institute, a fish-drying plant, and an office building have been planned; an emergency landing field is being prepared on Miquelon; before another year, a large pier will be begun for the trawler fleet. To supply electricity day and night, there will be a power plant on the hills and Le Frigo will be used to freeze fish again. Saint Pierrais look on in amazement. Some are enthusiastic, others are sceptical; a few of them are working very hard. All are thinking of the future.

The vice-president of Le Counseil General and manager of the fleet (two ships) looks and moves like a boss in American movies. He owns the theatre, the rink, a dance hall, a farm and summer home on Langlade, and the largest shop on the quay. He never leaves the colony. (It is whispered that if he goes to the mainland he will be nabbed by police for his activity during the rum-running days.)

He didn't talk to me, he shouted. "Saint Pierre-Miquelon will soon be top place for visitor in North America. On Langlade I will build a grand hotel and a casino bigger than Monte Carlo. Everyone will come to play the games and drink champagne, to dance, swim, and fish in the sea. In winter, skiing and Mardi Gras. Saint Pierre will be like night life in Paris."

Every morning Marcel Maxine comes to the quay. A good-looking young man with smiling blue eyes and a New-foundland mother, he throws rocks into the water to reinforce the wharf. "Dem big ones is hard work for we," he told me. "We got always too much to do at one time and none at de odder. In winter is only shovelling snow."

He looked wistfully at the boats in the harbour. "Don't you tink Canada should take all dis like she take Newfoundland? When schooner come in I go on board and listen to fishermen talk. Dey got more money now dat dey got Canada. I like to go dere to see what is like but I'm French and I got no trade. Can't git trade in Saint Pierre." He shrugged his shoulders and smiled. "You go to café? Every night I go. Notting else to do in Saint Pierre. Too much drink, not good, but plenty fun, eh?"

I stayed two weeks in Saint Pierre and could have enjoyed myself longer. People smiled at me shyly and some stopped to talk – they loved to practise their English, to laugh at my grop-ing French. They drove me from one end of their eighteen miles of road to the other and showed me three subsidized fox farms; they invited me to their homes for a glass of wine and a chat.

The Baslés live over on Gallantry Point in a very small house by the sea. They gave me tea with bread and cheese and paté. Jean-Baptiste was lightkeeper – he retired not long ago – and they live on a pension and fishing. Their son is a carpenter and earns forty francs an hour. They're hoping to find enough dollars one day to smuggle in a bow for his fiddle. They wrapped up two fine fat mackerel for me to take along for my dinner. Let me pay? "Oh, no, mam'selle, it is such a pleasure to have a visitor from the world."

One evening the St. John's football team came to Mme Dutin's for dinner. Marianne, in charming French custom, put her arms lightly around the captain's neck and touched both his cheeks with her lips. A shout went up from the rest of the team and the captain, of course, was transported. "I've never met people like these Saint Pierrais," he glowed. "They'd give you anything. In the cafés they treat us to drinks, they won't let us spend any money, they gave us a dance in the Great Hall, they're paying our board for an extra day and when we won a game they cheered louder than when they beat us."

One day I voyaged in the *Béarn* to the lonely village of Miquelon, which was established by Acadians in 1755. It is twenty-five miles from Saint Pierre, at the northern end of Miquelon Island on a flat strip of low land between two seas whose winds and tides and fogs try to obliterate it.

The five hundred people live there as their forefathers did – every family fishing, cultivating a sliver of land, and raising a few animals. Their ancient houses and connecting barns stretch out in two long rows separated by a muddy, grassy sort of boulevard with gardens down the centre closely fenced by unpeeled saplings to keep out the goats and dogs and fowls that wander everywhere. Fishing cabins stand on a parallel strip of beach where dories are drawn up by capstans and codfish are dried on the stones. The young Miquelonnais love to visit Saint Pierre but the older ones piously say it is much too wicked.

Women in Saint Pierre devote their lives to their families: they cook and clean and sew. There are no clubs, no beauty cults to distract them. They go to mass every morning. When they are old, they look out their windows with lonely curiosity. If their husbands or children have died they will wear black forever and visit very often the strange cemetery on the hill. Reverently they wander on the well-raked paths between the rows of new and ancient graves, each covered by a cement tomb with a cross raised high. On some are laid flowers of porcelain; on others wreaths of waxed paper rattle in the wind. Ships' port hole windows and wooden doors swing out from a number of vaults, and from the flower-decked coffins inside, the musty smell of death affronts the clear, cool air.

When a funeral procession slowly climbs the hill, it is led by a cross with a black banner waving over the man who carries it. A priest follows, chanting, then the hearse, a black delivery truck hung with bright paper flowers. Behind it a crowd of sad and silent people walk with bowed heads; in their midst on a staff someone carries a large French flag.

On the day before I had to leave Saint Pierre I ran round to say good-bye to some of the people I'd met. Over a glass of wine, Olympe and Gabrielle spoke of nothing but getting married and "having real soon the kids." Behind the bar in the Café du Nord, Mme Flahaut poured drinks of all sizes.

"Beezness ees good when trawlaire come in." Saint Pierrais Café du Nord, Madame Flahaut poured drinks of all sizes. "Beezness ees good when trawlaire come in." Saint Pierrais welcome the men from France; they strengthen the bonds between the two lands. In the Banque Andrieuv, Monsieur Andrieuv is one of the busiest men in the colony – he often has a meeting at five and another at seven – but he takes time to fill glasses of wine to wish me *bon voyage*. Alfred Gautier stops his roaring old truck beside me on the quay and begs me to stay longer. "Is big dance tomorrow night, you come wis me. More fun than all the time same Saint Pierre girl."

As I stood on the deck of the freighter that took me away from Saint Pierre I regretfully watched the little town fading softly into its mists. A French warship on a routine visit had anchored at the island. Red pompoms on the berets of its sailors enlivened the cafés; hearts fluttered when a naval officer crossed the quay. And in the Great Hall (once a liquor warehouse) the governor and his lady, the civil servant and his wife, the fishermen, Alfred Gautier and his girl, that evening would be dancing the samba, the tango, the twirling French waltz with champagne sparkling on every table.

Maclean's, April, 1950

In September 1971 I returned to Saint Pierre. Trawlers were tied rail to rail in the harbour; other ships waited to dock at the new government piers; port traffic was averaging thirteen hundred calls a year. The cafés and Mme Dutin's restaurant were thronged with fishermen from Spain, Russia, Germany, Portugal, Poland, Japan, Italy, and France.

Ten years later, in October, I flew to Saint Pierre. There were no ships in the harbour! Canada's two-hundred-mile limit was keeping foreign vessels away. Three Saint Pierre trawlers came in to have their fish processed at the new commercial fish plant and only thirty dories of local inshore fishermen were drawn up on the beaches. I was told, "The men get their quota early in the season and have no work for the rest of the year."

But despite inactivity on the waterfront, Saint Pierre had an air of prosperity. There were new buildings round the quay. In the narrow streets pedestrians were dodging Renaults, Peugeots, Citroëns, Datsuns, American compacts, taxis, and trucks. A car was parked in front of almost every house.

The once-drab wood-shingle houses were freshly and brightly painted. All round the perimeter of the town of five thousand people were larger new homes with picket fences enclosing front-yard vegetable gardens grown on soil imported from France.

I was told every house has a telephone, and that people can dial directly to France. Television programs are beamed in from the homeland and most people have additional TV sets to get Canadian programs as well. Electricity is no longer turned off at midnight.

Saint Pierre's stores have been enlarged to sell clothing, books, perfumes, and furnishings from France, and groceries from Canada. There were line-ups at bakeries with crusty French loaves and *patisseries* as delicate and delicious as any in Paris. *Tabac* and liquor stores had intriguing displays, but bottles were not the incredible bargain they used to be.

Restaurants in Saint Pierre posted tempting French menus. Mme Dutin, now eighty, still makes gourmet meals while Marianne charms the clientele as she waits on the tables. They proudly show copies of *Gourmet* magazine, *Reader's Digest*, and *National Geographic*, which praised madame's cuisine, and pictures of Pierre and Margaret Trudeau enjoying a meal with the territory's governor.

I was told that thousands of tourists come every summer to Saint Pierre on cruise ships or on planes; some drive to Newfoundland and come on the ferry from Fortune. They stay for a night or two in Saint Pierre's five hotels or in *pensions*; if they have no rooms, guests are welcomed in people's homes. Two travel agencies on la Place du General de Gaulle (formerly la Roncière) organize sea trips round the islands from May to September; they are even busier booking holidays for the Saint Pierrais. "Everyone saves money to go abroad at least once a year," I was told. "To France, the French Caribbean, New York, Montreal, or skiing in the Laurentians."

The University of Toronto and Newfoundland's Memorial University have as many as three hundred students going to St. Christoff's College to learn French throughout the summer. The students live with the people. (Fifteen female students have married Saint Pierrais and stayed; male students have taken French brides back to Canada.)

Young people gather in the evenings at the cafés and discos, or any hour in a youth centre with a large heated swimming pool, a theatre for movies, local theatricals and Basque dancing, a gymnasium, a library, a lounge, and rooms for craft classes. A museum on a back street boasts two thousand visitors a year.

On my October weekend in Saint Pierre I walked round the town in the wind and the rain. Most of the older people who'd entertained me on my first visit were gone: M. Landry, more than eighty, was on a visit in France. Mme Dutin was visiting her son in Halifax. Marianne invited me for dinner and showed me the fine modern house she has built for her retirement.

Ten minutes before the taxi came to drive me to the airport, the young man who had taken me dancing long ago came to greet me. "I just hear you were in Saint Pierre." He kissed me on both cheeks. "You remember? You remember?" He asked me about many things. I remembered.

He told me he has a wife and five sons. "Me, very good at making boys." He grinned. "And good living, driving car for governor. France looks after Saint Pierre very well," he said. "Not so much champagne now, too expensive. But still plenty fun. Why you don't stay longer?" And he kissed me again – in the manner of a true Frenchman.

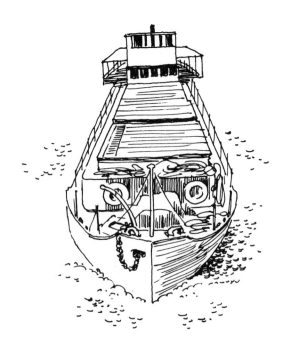

The Boats That Sail a Warpath

*B*ecause my story about the Old Order
Mennonites won the Canadian Women's Press
Club Award in 1950, the editors at *Maclean's* were
anxious to get me started on another piece. Within a
week I was on my way to Donnacona, Quebec, to
board a canal barge carrying newsprint to New York
City via the inland waterway up the St. Lawrence
and Richelieu Rivers, through the Chambly Canal,
Lake Champlain, and the Hudson River, a tranquil
scenic trip past old Indian battlegrounds. No one
knew it would end in tragedy.

A lmost every day, from spring breakup to winter freezing, a peculiar little freighter with a crew of *Canadiens* leaves the paper-mill town of Donnacona, on the north shore of the St. Lawrence just above Quebec City, to take two hundred thirty tons of newsprint to New York by way of an old Indian warpath. Always close to a friendly shore and safe from stormy seas, the boat passes a chain of forts built by the French to repel the Iroquois and the English. It sails by quiet fields and sleepy Quebec villages, the Green Mountains of Vermont, the Catskills and Palisades. It passes Three Rivers, Sorel, West Point, a nudist camp, Sing-Sing prison, and the Statue of Liberty.

The trip south takes three days and three nights. A tree growing in the Laurentians can become a newspaper in Times Square in less than a week. The crew has fun in New York while the boat is reloaded, then through the land of the Mohawks they return with bags of Spanish paprika, green coffee, desiccated coconut, Japanese sewing machines, antimony ashtrays, and rayon teddy bears.

Six identical barges of the Donnacona Paper Company – and one used by the Gatineau Paper Company – are the only vessels carrying cargo along the route that cuts the distance between Montreal and New York from 1,670 miles by sea to 452 miles by way of the St. Lawrence and Richelieu Rivers, Lake Champlain, and the Hudson. Straight, narrow, and flat, the boats were designed to fit, like a finger in a glove, the nine small locks of the Chambly Canal which, in a charming but obsolete way, circumvents the rapids of the Richelieu.

They are so carefully weighted that one extra roll of newsprint might ground them in the sixty-six miles of shallow water north of the American border. Their wheel-houses, smokestacks, and masts are detachable so the boats can pass under the low bridges of the Champlain Canal, which connects the narrows of Lake Champlain with the upper reaches of the Hudson. Wherever they pass people stop to stare.

It was midnight when I went aboard the *Newscarrier*, which was waiting at the pier in Donnacona for the tide to launch her voyage. Though I was there to write about the trip, I was listed in the ship's articles as second cook. Captain Armand

Normandeau, a shy little man nearing fifty, showed me the quarters I was to share with her crew of seven. At the back of the vessel, in a space the size of an average-size living room, were four cabins, a galley, a washroom hung with lilac deodorizers, a companionway and ventilators from the engine room, two passageways, and stairs to the wheelhouse – all as compact as a doll's house.

"We make for you a place with the cook, my daughter Rollande." The captain introduced a small, pretty young woman in one of the tiny cabins. She spoke no English; I understood very little French. Without a word, she took off her dressing gown and her red satin slippers, then climbed into her berth to make room for me and my luggage.

My makeshift bunk was eighteen inches below the ceiling; from its trough I stretched out my arm to flip off the light switch on the wall across the room. The diesel below us began to throb. Through the porthole beside my pillow I watched mountains of pulpwood fade in the darkness. The *Newscarrier* moved southwest up the St. Lawrence. We slept; Rollande's alarm clock roused us at five in the morning.

At Sorel, forty-six miles below Montreal and ninety-four above Donnacona, we turned south into the Richelieu, the main line of warfare in the long-ago struggle for supremacy in America. We saw a great armament plant, freighters taking on cargo, passenger ships at anchor, a ghost fleet of minesweepers with flaking grey paint, then *canadien* farmhouses, gracious stone *manoirs*, and new little houses built like all the new little houses everywhere in Canada.

On the *Newscarrier* the narrow deck around the three hatches was being scrubbed by a stocky young man wearing a tuque with a bobbing pompom. Thrusting out his broom, he struck an operatic pose and burst into *La Traviata*. "That's Roger, my deckhand." The captain laughed. "He's *bouffon*."

The watch changed every six hours. At noon the captain was relieved by the mate, Josephat Hardy, forty, a man with blue eyes, a tuque on the back of his curly brown hair, and three tattoos on his arms. Adjutor du Four, forty-four, lively as a squirrel, took the place of Antoine Harvey, thirty-one, the darkly handsome chief engineer. Tall, athletic Leo Leclerc, seventeen, was the second deckhand. Rollande, always in the galley, served pea soup, boiled potatoes, steak, lettuce, and vs of chocolate layer cake covered with strawberry jam.

The engine sounded like a train going ninety miles an hour, but after passing through the modern lock at St. Ours, where the Richelieu is rocky, our boat was making less than half its maximum of twelve knots.

"Dis could be quick trip for many boat, but the government likes not to spend money here to raise up the river," Joe Hardy told me. "For fourteen mile from Sorel to St. Ours she is dredge but for other sixty-six mile to Lake Champlain, where is American border, she have only six and a half foot deep water. She have no buoys, no lights; we make our course by trees and houses. Sometime we go in the centre, sometime on one side, den on the other. You see dat first bridge ahead? We pass through right side of him; next bridge we go left. Is fine in day but night time or when is fog we do not always know. Last year dere is not many rains; near Chambly we are tied up to de bottom. We wait a few hour, then east wind bring water and we go off. But one time we wait six days."

Slowly we followed the river's curves, past St. Antoine, Vercheres, Beloiel, St. Hilaire. The men played cards, challenged one another to wrestle, and sang French songs. They pointed out Fort Chambly, overlooking Chambly Basin at the foot of the Richelieu rapids, where Indians once portaged their canoes and French, British, and American troops carried stores and ammunition on their way to battle.

Forty-six miles south of Sorel and twenty miles east of Montreal we reached the Chambly Canal. For miles the crew had been complaining about it – a channel thirty-six feet wide, only six and a half feet deep. It takes six hours to travel its length of twelve miles. It could be mistaken for a millrace except for its nine small locks (one hundred twenty by twenty-three feet). It was being constructed in 1831 at the time England and the United States were building their first steam railways. As soon as it was finished the government was entreated to improve it, and commissions have been petitioning governments ever since to modernize the bottleneck in the short cut between the largest city in Canada and the busiest city in the world.

"The Americans have spent many millions of dollars keeping their part of the waterway twelve feet deep," the commissioners report. "If the Chambly was modernized and the Richelieu dredged it would save life, fuel, money, and ships when there is war on the Atlantic. It would provide economical and speedy commercial traffic for a most productive area in Canada. It would make a perfect trip for vacationists." But commissions come and commissions go and the Chambly Canal remains exactly what it has always been – a narrow, shallow, picturesque ditch.

The *Newscarrier* was nuzzled into the first log-sided lock, with a six-inch clearance all around and under. We waited for the wooden gates to be wound open by hand, then moved into the next ancient lock and the next, forty-five feet above the basin where we'd entered. The men in the crew stepped out on the quay to do a bit of tussling. They tossed each other into the air and roared with laughter while a bridge on a main highway from Montreal was swung open and sixty-four cars waited for the *Newscarrier* to pass.

Our approach was telephoned to the next lock. When we passed through it the lock-keepers bicycled to the next one. Two men walked around a turnstile in the centre of a bridge to swing it open. Leo Leclerc sauntered along the tow path beside us.

In the wheelhouse Roger was saying, "We go not fast here; we touch bottom, mud and not big rocks. Every year dey dredge but the banks fall down. Now we pretty near stop."

The captain said, "She is stop."

The bow of the *Newscarrier* moved from side to side; the stern stuck.

"We don't worry," Roger said, "We do dat every trip, sometime five, six time same trip."

The *Newscarrier* was moving forward again. Soon the river was beside us, broad but shallow. The captain pointed. "You see over dere de dam? Dey build dat before de last war but dey spend all de money on de war and now dere is no money for de canal."

"Dey use have all kind of war round here with Injuns," Roger told me. "Dey fight with haxe and tommyhatch – don't need money for dat."

A lock and two bridges later we came to Lake Ste. Therese,

with summer camps on its shores. We crossed it in twenty minutes, then crawled between the canal's grassy banks.

"Dere is de home of my dreams," Roger said as we passed a Colonial house with a two-car garage. "But it will not be for me. I like too well dis job. Always it has something different: a few days in New York, a little beer and dancing the jitterboy, den back again to my wife. Nine months I work and save money, in winter I do nothing: read a book, listen to radio, play cards with my wife." He shrugged and grinned.

Whenever we came to a lock, Roger bounced across the hatches to throw the hawser over a bollard and to talk with the lock-keepers while they turned the archaic cranks. Darkness came as we moved through the laneway of water. There were dim lights along the tow path where horses used to draw wooden barges to be reloaded at either end of the canal. The navy-blue water ahead reflected fenceposts illumined by our searchlight.

At the town of St. Jean we came to the end of the canal. I went reluctantly to my bunk with a warning that I'd be roused at three o'clock, when we'd reach the American border. I was wakened by a light flashed in my face and a gruff voice demanding, "Do you belong to any Communist organizations? What magazines do you read? What dailies? What are you doing on this boat? Get out of bed and let me see your papers."

Next morning the Stars and Stripes was flying from our foremast. We were halfway down Lake Champlain. Roger, at the wheel, exulted in having deep water, but the little captain looked anxiously at a haze that dimmed the mountains beyond the shores. "Dis is bad lake in fog; got some rocks and islets." He took the wheel from Roger whenever an oil barge, five times as big as the *Newscarrier*, came towards us.

Before noon we were in the narrows of lower Lake Champlain, the mountains close on both sides, the channel edged with rushes. There was a feeling of Indians in ambush along the way.

"Three hundred year ago all dis is Canadian territories," Roger said. "Champlain is first white man coming here; he see Injuns at dis place and shoot off gun. Injuns never hear dat before and dey run. Mr. Champlain still stand dere near de bridge, can you see? Very nice statue."

While I was in the galley trying to talk with Rollande, Leo rushed down to fetch me. "Joe wants you see Ticonderoga."

"French built dat fort," Joe told me, "and dere Montcalm won last French victory over English before dey take Canada at Quebec."

Old stone walls faced our route, the route red-coated British soldiers and Yankee rebels had followed. We passed mansions with long green lawns, but most of the shore was wooded. The waterway grew narrower. The first low bridge of the Champlain Canal was in sight. The mate went down to steer from the lower wheelhouse. Roger and Leo took the roof off the upper one and slid it down on a hatch. The walls came off next, just like the flats for a stage, and they were carefully laid alongside the roof. Roger lowered the mast. Leo took down the stacks and the brass steering wheel. The upper wheelhouse lay on the deck. The *Newscarrier* was flat as a scow.

Whitehall, at the first of the canal's twelve locks, is a little town crowded between the mountains. "We got a lot of history around these parts," the lock-keeper told me. "Used to be a fort up there in the hills where Washington licked the English." A cannon pointed at us from the heights. A political speech blared from a passing sound car: "Vote Republican all the way." Rollande looked startled. All of us on the *Newscarrier* seemed suddenly very Canadian. Leo walked on the deck with the dignity of a king.

Captain Normandeau went ashore to buy fish for Friday. Joe got himself a pink ice-cream cone. Roger and Adjutor ran up the street.

"Going for a beer, boys?" Leo called after them.

Roger turned and piously rolled his eyes. "Not while we are working," he said.

The Champlain Canal's channel is deep and wide, its locks (three hundred feet by forty-five) fill quickly and are almost large enough for six boats like our little *Newscarrier*. We could navigate its sixty-eight miles in half a day.

"Not much boats but barges coming through now," the captain said. "In summertime is fine yachts from Hudson and Erie Canal going to Montreal, Saquenay, or Ottawa and the Lakes."

"Rich mans on dem wear white clothes, have pretty girls,

and fat seegar." Roger's gestures brought laughter and a burst of rapid French from the crew.

We were in the wheelhouse after supper. As always there was speculation about where we'd be at certain times along the way, when we'd meet another paper boat returning, what time we'd reach New York, and what cargo we'd bring back. Everyone hoped for package freight. "Takes longer to load and gives us more time in de city," Roger explained. "If we don't get dat we go to Jersey for phosphates, is dusty and it smells not good."

"We be in New York tomorrow night round nine o'clock," the captain said.

"And what will everyone do there?"

Rollande, I was told, would shop on Fourteenth Street; Joe liked the baseball; Adjutor stayed always on board; for Roger and the chief the Latin Quarter has many friends and night clubs; the captain would go to the shows. And Leo? He shrugged. "Too much peoples, I got friend girl in Donnacona," he said, "beautiful girl and good dancer." He hugged himself delightedly. "My gosh, I like to dance with my girl."

Our "last" day was the most glorious of all. When it came, bright and sunny, we were on the Hudson passing the Catskills. The crew frolicked and sang. A butterfly, large as a wren, flew along with the *Newscarrier*, soaring and fluttering. "Is good luck," the captain said.

When the new watch came on, the Hudson was broad as a lake and Leo had the wheel. Joe sat on the deck with me. "Dere is Bear Mountain Park" – he pointed – "where dey have de ski contest. Maple Leaf and Montreal baseball team practise dere too. One trip dis summer I bring along my little boy, take him to games in New York. He talk all de time since about dat." From his pocket Joe brought out a packet of pictures and showed me his lovely young wife, his little boy and girl, the new house he had built, his brother, who had died, ships he'd served on, icebergs, polar bears swimming, the dock at Donnacona.

We were passing a city of American ships used in the war, their hulls newly painted, waiting. Adjutor was on the deck singing a song to the tune of "O Holy Night." Men on an oil barge stared at us as they hurried by. "Dey don't see boat like dis before," said Joe. "She is different. Even in New York she is not like other boat but dere everybody is too busy to see. Dey go to work with breakfast in de pocket."

Joe brought out cards to play a game of casino with Adjutor on the hatch. I took their picture, then sat in the sun near them. Adjutor was pointing out the cars in the yard of the Chevrolet plant near Tarrytown. "Dey got more dan dey need," he said. "Could give me one."

Joe teasingly tossed water from a glass at Adjutor, who ran like a flash to the galley. We expected him to come up with a bucket of water to throw at Joe. Instead, he returned nonchalantly eating grapes. I was writing a letter, telling of this beautiful trip.

Suddenly Adjutor had turned Joe upside down and both men were screaming with laughter. Clutched in each other's arms they were tussling playfully at the edge of the hatch. I moved to get my camera on a bench by the wheelhouse, turned back to look at the men. They were gone! An iron post supporting the cable that ran round the edge of the deck was bent toward the water.

"They're *overboard!*" I screamed.

I looked for the men in the water. They had surfaced. I thanked God. Leo left the wheel to arouse the watch sleeping below. From the aft-deck, Rollande came toward me with terror in her eyes. "*Ne peuvent nager* [can't swim]," she cried.

Adjutor was splashing but his head was under. Joe was dog-paddling towards him. Leo had a boat hook in his hands but the men were beyond us.

Adjutor's splashing stopped; we could no longer see him. Joe was swimming alone towards the boat, which kept moving swiftly away from him, greatly lengthening the distance between. The men put down the anchor. Leo had a buoy ready to throw but Joe was too far behind us. In time that seemed endless – but was only minutes – the lifeboat was lowered from the stern. Roger and Leo rowed hard against the current.

Then we saw only the water. All water looks the same when there is nothing in it to see. I heard the chief engineer sobbing. There was anguish on the face of the little captain. Rollande held up two fingers and mournfully shook her head.

We kept watching the moving water, watching the men in

the boat who looked back at us with despair. There was nothing more we could do. The rowboat circled aimlessly in the wavelets. The caps of the drowned men lay on the hatch.

Roger and Leo came aboard. The *Newscarrier* was steered to the nearest wharf where a flashily dressed Negro and three little boys indignantly pulled in their fishing lines. The captain went ashore to notify the police. The rest of us paced on the hatches. Roger said, "Dis day I have lost my best friends." Leo told me, "Dese were two beautiful mans, always dey are chums and having de joke. Adjutor have wife and four children; dis summer his boy, eighteen year old, drown when he is swimming, and his wife's mother die too. Three die in two months."

Then there was action – police asking questions, townspeople staring, police taking pictures of Joe's tuque and Adjutor's denim cap on the hatch, the little captain searching the cold waters of the Hudson for another hour in a police boat, the ship's agents arriving from New York.

There was a ride to the police station in Tarrytown, waiting for a French interpreter, long questioning and written reports of Leo, Rollande, and I, who had seen the accident. The men from New York and the police talked about murders and racketeering on New York's waterfront. The little captain looked straight ahead, the lines on his strained face deepening.

At last it was over and they took us back to the boat. We'd eaten no supper and Rollande thought food might hearten us but only Leo ate, a bit of toast and a piece of cake.

We started again next morning. The flag in the bow was flying at half mast. There was no singing on the barge. We solemnly watched the waters of the Hudson.

The George Washington Bridge was just ahead and soon we saw Riverside Drive with its millionaires' yachts just below. Then came the piers with ships from Norway, Liverpool, Nantes, Le Havre, and Panama, where Joe had had the tattoo put on his left arm. We passed the *Queen Elizabeth* and the *Queen of Bermuda*. New York's skyline was lost in a haze. In a bewildering enigma of traffic, the little captain steered our canal barge steadily through the harbour, round the Battery, under the Brooklyn and Manhattan bridges to Pier 40 in the East River.

The *Newscarrier* had brought another load of paper from the forests of Quebec to the concrete wilderness of New York. The people in Times Square were already reading all about it. The men of the crew went ashore to phone home to Donnacona.

Maclean's, July 1, 1951

☆   ☆   ☆   ☆   ☆

On a sunny morning in late September, with a friend in my car, I found my way via the labyrinth of roads south and east of Montreal to the first lock of the Chambly Canal at Chambly Basin. Through a wire-mesh barrier we watched four pleasure craft approach the lock while two young men wound the ancient machinery that opened the gates. "Only for pleasure boats now, dis canal," we were told. "Not open day and night any more, only for twelve hour."

"What about the paper boats that used to come through here?"

The young men shrugged their shoulders. "We don't know about dem, no paper boats here now."

Along a road beside the canal we drove as far as St. Jean, where the canal ends. With trees and houses side by side along its west bank, the canal still resembles a tranquil, picturesque millrace.

Next day we drove along the St. Lawrence to Donnacona, where the paper mill, with its mountains of pulpwood, had been expanded to a tremendous complex of buildings owned by Domtar Limited. How could I ever find anyone I knew in that vast establishment?

Miraculously, a uniformed security guard had read my story in *Maclean's* thirty-one years ago; he directed me to the home of Leslie Palmer, who had been the general manager of the mill when I made my trip. From his files and his memory Mr. Palmer was able to tell me that most of the paper boats had stopped running in 1956, when customers in New York stopped buying Donnacona paper. The men

71

who had delivered the newsprint found other jobs on the river.

"The *Newscarrier* wasn't taken out of service until 1969, when she was sold to a Quebec river pilot, who in turn sold her to a firm doing wharf construction on the lower St. Lawrence. After being stripped of machinery the ship was used as a scow and eventually scrapped."

And what of the crew?

A week after they were drowned, the bodies of the mate and second engineer were found eight miles farther along the Hudson from where they fell in.

Captain Normandeau died in 1974 in his seventy-first year.

Chief Engineer Antoine Harvey was drowned in the Louise Basin port of Quebec in 1962 during the winter tie-up of the *Newscarrier*. He had left the ship to go ashore via planks and gangways laid over the ice. The final gangway to the wharf collapsed, and Antoine went through the ice and was drowned.

Rollande Normandeau, the cook, married a marine engineer and lives in her old family home.

Deckhand Leo Leclerc worked in the mill until he was forty-eight, when he suffered a heart attack and was forced to retire.

And Roger? I couldn't find out about Roger because I couldn't remember his last name – if I ever knew it. I wonder if he is living now in the colonial home of his dreams beside the Chambly Canal.

Maggie's Leaving Home

Writing a book about Neil's Harbour gave me a great excuse to return there every other summer to get more material.

"How about a piece for *Maclean's*?" Pierre asked me in 1951 when I told him I was going to Cape Breton for a few weeks.

I found the story in the fisherman's house where I always stay when I go back to the village: there, pretty little Maggie, one of the youngest of Henry and Clara May Ingraham's thirteen children, was preparing to leave her home by the sea for the glamour, wealth, and adventure she dreamed she would find in far-away Toronto.

M aggie Ingraham is leaving her home in Neil's Harbour, the secluded little fishing village down north on the Cabot Trail in Cape Breton. She is leaving the sea, the broad sky, and the highlands to get a job in Toronto. Maggie has never been farther than Sydney, a hundred-odd miles away. She is little and lively and twenty and she wants to see the world.

"I know I'll miss the salt water," she says, looking seaward, "and I'll make Mom and them all feel right bad, but the Harbour is always the same like, and I can't get nothin' more here."

The lure of the cities in the past three decades has changed Canada's population from 54 per cent to 46 per cent rural and Maggie is part of the pilgrimage from country to town that is as continual as the sailing of ships.

Like other restless young people who watch the roving tides from a lonely shore, like those who dream wildly where the wheatfields are golden, like the wistful ones whose eyes follow the stream of cars on the highways that cut through their farmlands and hamlets, like many who are curious and eager and daring enough, Maggie, in her rockbound harbour, is determined to seek her fortune far from the known ways of home.

While she listens to stories on the battery radio or to visitors from town, while she sees the shiny cars of the tourists who go around the Trail, Maggie imagines a life in the city that is warm and rich and exciting. And she chooses to go to Toronto, with its fabulous wealth and variety, with cocktail bars, Eaton's and Simpsons great stores, and her married sister Eva, whose letters tell that she loves city life but Neil's Harbour will always be home.

Bleached, windswept, and beautiful, Maggie Ingraham's village is almost surrounded by the blue of the North Atlantic. The jagged rims of its cliffs curve round to a rocky point where a red-capped white lighthouse rises against the sky. Scattered over the slopes of a treeless hill are a hundred little houses with gables pointing to the sea where the fishing boats come in.

Old men whittle in the sun by the grey shingle stages clustered around the shore. Young men sway on the masts of the swordfishing boats as they search for the precious prey. Cod-fishermen wearing rubber boots and trousers split their catch on the blood-encrusted jetties.

There is little movement in the village: the occasional flash of colour as a woman crosses a yard, the slow roaming of cows and horses outside the fences, the playing of children at the docks and on the roads. And there is little sound: only the whisper of the water, the calling of the birds, the moaning of the bell buoy.

No one is disturbed by a telephone ringing: there is no line into the village. Electric power is still on its way. The nearest high school is a hundred miles distant. Magazines and news-papers are not sold in Neil's Harbour. There are no super-markets to lure Maggie's mother from home – she does her shopping from the mail-order catalogues or by saying, "Philip, dear, run down to Archie's and get me a can of peas and anything fresh he's got in." In the fall her storehouse is filled with barrels of flour, sugar, salt herring, dried cod, frozen venison. "We has to save up in the busy months," she ex-plains, "because in winter there's no way of earning a cent till the boys catches seals off the drift ice."

There is little for Maggie to buy in the three little shops of the village. She has been saving her earnings to leave the life that is tranquil and sure for one that is startling and new. For a year she's been a nurses' aid and cook at Neil's Harbour's one-doctor, eight-bed Red Cross hospital, a place of delivery and relief for all the pregnancies and emergencies along sixty miles of coast. The twelve-hour duty is strenuous; there are six half-days off in a month, and the job pays fifty-eight dollars. It is the only available work for a girl who lives in Neil's Harbour, unless she wants to clean lobsters in season (May 15 to July 15) for eighteen cents an hour. Maggie hopes to make eighty dollars a month when she finds something to do in the city.

"And every week I'll send home a present for somebody," she promises her family.

Maggie is fifth youngest of her mother's thirteen children. Matt, Fred, John, and Jean have homes of their own in the village; Annie and her family live in Sydney Mines, Martha in Glace Bay; Eva, with her husband and baby, have two rooms in Toronto, and Norman's away in the army because he wants to travel. The rest of the Ingrahams live in the brown-shingle house on the hill in Neil's Harbour.

On a windy mid-July morning, Henry, the father, hauls the last of his lobster traps for the season. Ewart, twenty-three, carries home a codfish by the tail for dinner before he returns to the shore to play poker. Bobbie, seventeen, milks Cherry, the freckle-rumped cow with the "government-tested" clip in her ear. Both boys are sharesmen of Fred's whose boat they've made ready for swordfishing. Lillian, seven, plays with her nephew, little Reid, near the woodpile. Philip, thirteen, reluctantly draws buckets of water from the well. In the kitchen on the lounge behind the stove, plump little Alf Budge, eighty-one, from next door, wearing a red plaid shirt and a quarter inch of whiskers, is smoking his pipe and chewing. Jean and her baby have come in for a pickle jar of milk. Above the whir of the gasoline-operated washing machine, Clara May, Maggie's mother, is screaming, "Go darn these socks, they got as many holes into 'em as a herrin' net. And look at Ewart's shirt, his best one, put it on last night and went and launched a boat, now it's roight beat up."

Maggie, off night duty at seven, comes through the back door. "Soon I'll be goin' on a train for two days and two nights," she says gaily.

"Uh, uh," grunts the old man on the lounge, "it's a long ride fer yer first one."

"I'm not goin' to sleep all the way so I won't miss none of the sights." Maggie snatches the striped denim cap off old Alf's head, puts it on her own and pretends she is engineering. "Choo-choo! Lily, watch out or I'll run over you and the cat." She peers out of an imagined cab. "I wants to see what it's like when we leave Cape Breton and crosses over to Nova Scotia."

Maggie is merry and mad and impulsive; everyone waits for her coming so there will be laughter. Her restless *joie de vivre* can't be sustained in Neil's Harbour. The moment she enters the house she turns on the radio to a Cape Breton station that plays old-time music. "You got the money and I got the time," she sings and step-dances. She puts on a man's jacket and waves its long sleeves like a scarecrow.

"Maggie, now don't be so foolish," her mother calls. "Git on upstairs and paint the sills in the big boarder's bedroom. I've riz up the windows and took down the curtains."

As Maggie obeys she wistfully says, "It will be some strange to live in the city in a little small room by myself, in a house with no space around it."

The Ingrahams' house stands in the centre of a rocky field, the cow barn, pigpen, and privy in the front corner blocking the view of the lighthouse but not of the sea. Not a small house nor a large one, Clara May bought the front part for seven hundred dollars after her first husband died of illness from the First World War; the back half was Henry's and he moved it over from his brother's field and connected it up when he married Clara May.

At first it was only roughly finished but now every room has a door and is prettily papered. There are linoleum mats on birch floors, and the downstairs rooms have waist-high paneling of pine. The front room has a chesterfield and upholstered chairs, the dining room has a couch and two leatherette rockers as well as an oak table, chairs, and buffet, and a portrait of Clara May's first husband hanging above the radio. There are six double beds in five bedrooms upstairs.

All the rooms in the house are used but everyone likes to gather in the enormous kitchen to be with Clara May, whose heart is as warm and crackling with affection as the fire that burns in the shiny black stove. There is always someone sitting on the rocker or the wooden lounge built into the corner: there is always a grandchild begging for a cookie, always a neighbour on the chair beside the door of the closed porch where the water pails and rubber boots are kept. The kitchen looks like a baby clinic when the young mothers come with their little ones to call for their daily pint of milk.

"In town all you need do is put a ticket in a bottle outside your door and a man brings you your milk," Maggie tells them.

"For all that, I wouldn't want to do without my old cow," Clara May says fondly, "she's that noice and koind. Henry's got to sharpen the scythe and make hay for her one o' these days."

"Eva wrote I better get Dad to cobble all my shoes that needs it before I go," Maggie says.

"I guess you won't foind a man so handy as him in town," Clara May observes drily.

Like most men in Neil's Harbour, where there are no

specialists, Henry can do almost anything. He gets up at three in the morning and goes fishing till ten or eleven. He makes wheelbarrows and dories, he fixes locks, he chops wood, he does carpentry, painting, and papering, he goes hunting and lumbering, he works on the roads. Throughout the day he shambles in and out of the house and down to the shore with a smile as enigmatic and perpetual as Mona Lisa's.

"But if that man knows there's a haircuttin' to do he'd do it 'stead of earnin', he's that crazy for it," Clara May declares. In the Ingraham kitchen, the yard, or the cow barn – wherever is most convenient – Henry safety-pins an old khaki coat round the neck of whoever comes for a clipping. His skill in the barberless village has a reputation. "He never finished Reid's hair though," Clara May says. "Got half done and stopped to empty the pail of slops under the sink and the choild hasn't let him get handy to him since. Henry's give him soda pop and tatie chips but he won't let him near with the scissor. He's been runnin' round fer a week now with 'is head just half cut."

"I might learn hairdressin'," Maggie speculates. "They pay money for a haircut in town."

"You better stick to housework," Clara May advises. "That's what you knows how to do."

Maggie scowls. "I'd rather go in a factory, you don't got to work so long."

"Work won't hurt you, you'll never git sick while you've somethin' to do and someone to do for," says Clara May, whose work for her family is never done. Unlike the city housewife, who has electricity and plumbing to make life easy, she gets up at five every morning, starts the fire and cooks porridge, bacon, and eggs for the boarders who work on the roads and the boys who go fishing. She bottles the milk and looks after the hens, grumbling, "The broody old sluts always lays away if I don't bar 'em up." Before she starts washing, scrubbing, or sweeping her always spotless house, she makes pies or bran muffins and cake. Twice a week she bakes bread. "They loike the homemade so much better'n what the truck brings from town," she says. "That baker's stuff don't seem to last no time inside 'em when they's out on the water. Henry, git me some chips, there ain't a livin' spark in the stove."

There is always a good smell of cooking when the fire burns bright. Cod, mackerel, herring, haddock, halibut, salmon, and lobster are an hour from the cold salt water. Roast chicken is a favourite and corned beef is convenient; frozen meat is often ordered from the little general store. Fresh vegetables are scarce, greens seldom seen; fresh fruits in season are bought by the dozen but berries can be picked on the barrens by anyone feeling inclined.

"Soon I'll just have to sit in a restaurant and order whatever I like." Maggie lights a cigarette like a grande dame. "I'm goin' to tell 'em my name is Marguerite," she says impishly, "or should I change it to Bernadette?"

"Oh, Maggie, don't talk so. I don't know how we'll get on without you," her mother laments.

A twinge crosses Maggie's face. "I'll make lots o' money and send Lily a dress and I'll get ties for Ewart and Dad straight out of Eaton's and Simpsons." Maggie dances around the room. "And I'll buy myself a formal and go to a New Year's ball in a big high building like we seen in the pitchers."

"You'll git lonesome when you ain't handy to home," Ewart tells her as he shaves off his weekly whiskers at the kitchen sink.

"No, I won't. Eva and Richard and others from the Harbour's up there, there's lots o' Cape Bretoners in Toronto, they has a dance for 'em every month. Why don't you come too, Ewart? We could get a place together."

Ewart shakes his head. "I'd rather stay where I'm at and go fishin'."

Maggie grabs him and they swing to the radio's country music. Bobbie swings with Lily, Clara May swings Philip, and they all laugh with breathless delight.

"Truck goin' ower to Dingwall tonight for a dance," says old Alf.

Clara May protests, "They can't spend money for that, they got just as good times in their own place. Bobby Fricker plays the guitar loud as any I heard and Herman's right smart on the fiddle."

"But I loves to drive in a car." Maggie's eyes are gleaming. "When I gets up there to Ontario maybe I'll get some rides; everybody there's got cars."

"There's cars in Cape Breton too." Clara May is defensive. "You knows that just last week Mr. Lolly came over from Ingonish and took Lil and me to Dingwall. We had the grandest droive, went roight down to the sand; then we stopped at a restaurant at Cape North – just as noice as any you'd see in town – and he bought us a banana split." She paused ecstatically. "Moi dear Lord, I does love a banana split."

"It'll be a long time before you get a drive to Cape North for another one," Maggie says. "Cars ain't that plenty around here."

Though all the fishermen own or share a boat with a motor, only four people in the village have a car: the preacher, the doctor, fisherman Kootch Fricker, and Sam Foss, who runs a canteen. When there is a dance in Ingonish or Dingwall, twelve miles either way from Neil's Harbour, the young people pay a dollar a trip to ride in the back of a truck.

"You goin' to dance, Alf?" Maggie asks the old man.

He looks surprised and says, "If my legs wasn't bad I'd take you. Ain't been to a dance in seventy year."

Ewart says, "You was too, you ain't that old. I'm only twenty-three and I remembers the time you fell over the bank behind Day's."

The old man uncomfortably rubs his hand across his long yellowed moustache and shakes his head, "No, no."

"Yis you was," Ewart persists, "I seen you."

Henry, blissfully riding Lily and a grandchild on the rocker, says, "They had to haul 'im up with a rope."

Ewart goes on. "You ain't so old or so bad off as you makes out; you's just as smart as we is if you wants to be. If you had a quart o' rum in you you'd be good at a dance as ever you was."

"You thinks I looks good, you thinks I's fat," the old man says, "but I ain't, I's swole." He gets up indignantly and walks out of the house.

"Ewart, you shouldn't tease the pore old man," Clara May says fondly, "it's a sin, that's what it is, it's a sin."

Henry grins. "Did you see the bottle sticking out his back pocket?"

After supper the old men of Neil's Harbour go to the shore to learn the latest news. The children wait on the dock for the swordfishing boats to come in. A little crowd gathers at Foss's for ice-cream cones and pop. One night a week there's a double showing of moving pictures in the hall of the Orange Lodge.

The most popular pastime at dusk is to walk up and down the road. Groups of boys sit on the grassy banks and whistle and call to the girls who pass by. Sometimes they follow the girls and clasp them or they walk with them to the rocky slopes above the sea and smoke a cigarette. Sometimes there's a roast on the sand beach where the daring ones have a swim.

There's a dance twice a month in the Legion Hall, where a rule forbidding swearing and fighting is strictly enforced. The bar in the corner sells Iron Brew, root beer, and Coke. The nearest liquor store is sixty miles away but sometimes the boys go to Dingwall and get a bottle off a schooner to drink behind the bushes before they crowd into the hall where the benches around the walls are solid with women and girls and there's room for five squares on the floor.

"Oi guess you'll git nothin' but round dancin' in town," a girl says to Maggie as she steps up to her partner.

"I loves that," says Maggie who's been twirling all night in the sets.

Most of Maggie's friends who have stayed in Neil's Harbour are married and having a baby every year, but they don't miss the dances – though their husbands sometimes stay home. Maggie walks home with them in the darkness: past the Anglican church and the schoolhouse, beside the rocky high banks of the sea towards the yellow flame of the lighthouse, up the winding hill to the Ingraham house where a lamp burns all night at the top of the stairs. Maggie's busy little body isn't still for a moment till she kneels in prayer at the side of her bed.

On the morning of Maggie's departure the sun shines – on the prairies, the highways, and all the quiet little places where venturesome youngsters leave home. It shines bright in Neil's Harbour. Lines from lobster traps are hanging over the fence rails to dry; bobbers and killicks are piled on the shore. Fishermen paint hulls and fix engines. A swordfish was brought in last evening and excitement in the village is high. The snapper boats have been launched and the men are going out on the sea.

Two brand-new travelling bags labelled TORONTO are waiting in the Ingrahams' front hall. The family is in the kitchen round the breakfast table. Henry sips his tea and says, "It was quite a family when all thirteen was at home. We used to need twelve barrels of flour in a year, now we'll only need four."

"Ewart thinks Maggie will be home again, don't you, Ewart?" Clara May asks hopefully.

"Lots went away and came back to Cape Breton," Ewart consoles her.

"I won't till I got a car," says Maggie. "Unless I come home for Christmas."

Getting up and looking at the sea Ewart says, "It blows harder outside than it does in handy."

"I ain't scared." Maggie's eyes are brightly excited.

Ewart puts on his swordfishing cap and walks to the door. "Well, so long," he says to the sister he loves best of anyone in the world.

"So long," says Maggie.

Clara May shouts, "Maggie, you eat your breakfast. Do you want to starve to death on the way?"

Maggie asks quickly, "You goin' fishin' now too, Bobbie?"

"Yes, so long."

"So long."

Clara May's eyes fill with tears and she stays by the front-room window as Henry and Philip and Jean go down the hill to the bus that will carry Maggie away.

When Ewart came home for supper that night he shivered and said, "It seems just like a fall day, don't it?" And Henry, when he came, said the same.

Maclean's, November 1, 1951

People keep asking me: "Whatever happened to Maggie? How did she get along in the city?"

She did very well. She got a job as a housekeeper, worked for a year or so, sent presents home, met

Ray, a handsome young man in the Air Force, and married him.

Throughout the years Ray had postings in various parts of Canada and Maggie enjoyed living wherever they went. She had three sons to take care of, and whenever Ray had a leave they drove back to Neil's Harbour. "The boys love fishing and playing with all their cousins," Maggie said. "Ray loves it too, and I can catch up on the gossip."

When Maggie's father died Ray retired from the Air Force and they went back to Neil's Harbour to stay. Ray got a job as warden in Cape Breton's national park. The boys went to school in the village and are now doing well at university in Antigonish. Maggie knits them Fair Isle sweaters and feeds them great meals when they come home on weekends.

Maggie is still lively, happy, and fun. After Clara May died in 1976, Maggie transformed the old house with broadloom and modern furnishings. "But everyone comes and sits in the kitchen just like we always did when Mom was around. We're all back home again," Maggie rejoices. "Eva's back from Toronto, so's Martie, Ewart, Norman, Freddie. Only Philip is away, and he can hardly wait to retire and come home."

The Lord Will Take Care of Us

"*H*ow would you like to go out to a Hutterite colony in southern Alberta?" Pierre asked me one day in the summer of 1951.

I was thrilled; I'd never been west of Ontario.

Pierre said, "I've read that none of the Hutterites are ever sent to mental or penal institutions, and it would be interesting to know why."

I knew nothing about Hutterites. I went to the Kitchener public library to read all I could. Then I got on a train bound for Lethbridge; from there I took a bus for Waterton Lakes to see mountains and to try to find a Hutterite colony. My seat companion was an older woman who warned me to have nothing to do with the Hutterites. "We don't think much of them around here." She elaborated disparagingly; I was glad when she left me.

Across the aisle was a pretty young woman with a little boy. She was talking to the bus driver and I couldn't help overhearing.

"Pardon me for eavesdropping," I said to her. "Are you living on a Hutterite colony?"

"I'm the teacher at the Old Elm," she said, and I told her why I was interested.

"If you'll come to the drug store in Magrath on Saturday night just before seven o'clock, you can come with me," she said. "A couple of young Hutterite boys will be driving into town to pick us up and take us to the cabin they provide for the teacher on the colony. There's an extra cot and you're welcome to stay with me until Wednesday – that's when my husband is coming back from a Mormon mission on the east coast. I haven't seen him for more than a year and I want to be with him alone." She grinned. "But by that time you may have got acquainted with some of the people and talked them into letting you stay with them."

A group of scientists recently made the astonishing discovery that while every tenth person in Canada suffers from mental illness or nervous disability, the Hutterites, in their communal colonies, are almost entirely free of both. In southern Alberta, where more than half the world's eight thousand Hutterites live, I visited a colony that was like a mediaeval retreat from the twentieth century.

Of the same pacifist origin as the Mennonites and Quakers, the Hutterites preserve similar traditions except they do not believe in individual ownership. As many as two hundred Hutterites live together like one happy family in a colony. They own all property in common; each person is allotted what he or she needs and everyone shares alike. They grow their own food, spin their wool for socks – they won't wear sweaters because their ancestors didn't – they make their own buildings, furniture, clothing, high-buttoned shoes, and wine. They all eat together in a communal dining room. Their houses contain only bedrooms, divided into family units: one room for a family of six or less, two or three rooms if a family is larger or the boys and girls are growing up.

The management of a colony is in the hands of the baptized men. Every job is assigned by vote: the preacher, elected from among the people, is the head but he works on the farm like the rest; the boss is the business manager, though nothing can be bought or sold without voting; the farm boss details the daily tasks to the men who have no specific jobs. There are also a carpenter, a tanner, a stock-and-poultry man, a shoemaker, and a German schoolteacher. All work is divided equally. No one receives any wages and everyone praises the Lord.

Though never interfering with other people, the Hutterites have had to learn how to take persecution. In 1536, when Jacob Huter, their founder, was burned at the stake, they fled from the Tyrol to Hungary, then to Rumania, later to Russia, and in 1874 to the United States where they had trouble avoiding the draft in the First World War. The Canadian government encouraged them to come to Canada by promising exemption from military service (the government rescinded the pledge a year later). A few groups stayed in South Dakota; the rest bought bald prairie in Alberta and Manitoba.

Because they increased and prospered, kept aloof from the towns, wouldn't vote, take oaths, or bear arms, neighbours and tradespeople resented them. Accordingly, in 1943, the Alberta legislature made it illegal for Hutterites to buy property within forty miles of another colony and for any one colony to buy more than six sections of land anywhere in the province. Manitoba considered passing a similar law but decided it was undemocratic.

There are now more than fifty Hutterite colonies in Alberta, in Manitoba about twenty. They are autonomous but united by their beliefs, and by an annual consultation of preachers, by intercolony visits, and by marriage.

I stayed for more than a week at the Old Elm Colony, thirty miles south of Lethbridge and eleven miles from Magrath, the nearest prairie town. The collection of green-trimmed white-and-red buildings was like a tidy hamlet. Among its hundred and fifty Hutterites there were only five surnames: Wurtz, Kleinsasser, Waldner, Decker, and Wipf. When I complimented them on their impressive reputation for mental health they modestly claimed to be much too mortal to deserve it: the boss, John Wipf, was having a nervous breakdown from worry because the colony couldn't buy more land to start a new colony.

Sunday was my first day on the colony. Its dawn did not come quietly; it came with the honking roar of eight hundred geese and the ringing of a bell on the roof of the dining hall.

While I listened to the drone of singing in the church, which was also the schoolhouse, a flock of toddlers and girls carrying babies discovered me. Dressed like the grownups in long skirts and plaid aprons, their hair severely drawn under tight bonnets or white-dotted black kerchiefs, the baby minders looked as if they were playing mother. To them a stranger on the colony was as exciting and curious as a castaway to the natives of a lonely island.

"My gosh, but I like you," Lydia Kleinsasser announced at first sight.

"You haf nize clothes," little Benny Wurtz said shyly.

"And that's for sure," several others agreed.

"Why do you wear dis ting?" they asked about my bracelet. They asked me my age. They asked dozens of questions about where I had come from. They gave me a carrot to eat. They posed while I took their pictures and begged me to take more, though picture-taking is supposed to be sinful. They showed me around the colony.

We went first to the building with the dining room, the bakery, and the cement-floored kitchen with its propane stoves, then to the wash-house where the women take turns doing their own family's laundry. We went to a pond to watch a thousand snowy ducks. "We got more dan dem yet but dey're in a freeze locker in town," the children told me. They showed me a pen for hundreds of pigs, a model barn where thirty cows are milked by machine, a spotless white dairy, painted barns for nine hundred sheep, sixteen hundred chickens, a hundred sixty horses. They pointed out the workshops, the granary with bins for thousands of bushels, the sheds for trucks, combines, tractors, threshing machines, and binders. "And we got fourteen acres of garden yet," the little girls said. "And we haf two sections in pasture for cattle and seven nearly all in grain." The little ones reminded me that the smallest member of a Hutterite colony is an owner of all its wealth.

In the shade of a long white building two couples with babies sat on little painted stools. The women's faces were plain, their eyes bright. One man was fair and placid; the other, ruddy and handsome, looked too cynical for his Hutterite clothes and the beard that showed he was married. "These damn whiskers interfere with my collar," he said, irritably running his finger under the neckband. "I wear them as short as I dare."

We chatted a while then he told me, "I left the colony once as some fellows do when they're young and unquiet and want to know what it's like to be out in the world." He restlessly picked up a pebble and flicked it at a passing goose. "I found out," he said, and his tone was bitter. "I got around. I dressed in suits with padded shoulders, I talked to a lot of guys. And women," he added with a snort while the woman beside him complacently husked a sunflower seed and put it into her mouth.

"I came back," the man said with his sardonic smile and a nod at his wife. "I came back to her." He picked up their tiny

90

daughter, sat her on his knee, and kissed the back of her neck under the frill of her bonnet. "Colony women are true," he said softly, "ain't they, my *froschlein*?"

"I never was tempted yet to go away," the other young father told me. "If we leaf the colony we got nothing but the clothes we walk out in and when I figger how it would be if I had to look for a job and maybe not ged one, I'm scared already." He shook his head. "So far I got only three kits, but if I was in the world and hat more kits the money I'd make would haf to stretch thinner and thinner for all; on the colony each kit gets what it needs no matter how many we haf."

"We don't take baby bonus or pension from the country," one of the wives said with a touch of pride. "We live here with our own people that believe the same as we do and when we are old or sick they'll take care of us. We never have nothing to worry over."

"If we want a doctor or to go to the Mayo Clinic in Minnesota we have just to ask and they give us the money," said the handsome man.

"But there's a bonesetter of our own people that knows more than some of the doctors in town," his wife said.

The other woman brought chokecherry wine from the house. "We drink to your friendship," she said, and drained a glass of its mildness.

"The boss gives us a gallon a month," the fair man said. "We get everything by allotment: every year a new hat and a pair of shoes, every five years a sheepskin coat. Every man over fourteen is given a dollar a month to spend – within our rules."

"What about the women?" I asked.

"They don't get any money but when a girl is fourteen she is given a chest for her clothes, a rolling pin, and a spinning wheel. When she's married she gets a sleep bench, a sewing machine, a wall clock, table and chairs, and the big books of Hutterite history."

"Come in our house once and see," the woman invited.

Their "house" in the long, low, gabled building that held eight families was one room, eighteen feet square. The hardwood floor shone like a table top. The furniture around the gleaming white walls was the colour of wheat, dowelled and dovetailed without the use of a nail; flowers were painted on the big feather bed and the chests. The counterpane and wall mottoes were embroidered in colourful cross-stitch.

The man demonstrated the sleep bench: like a chest with arms and back, the lid lifted up and the front pulled out making room inside for the children to sleep on plaid-covered feather-filled bedding. The wife showed me a chest full of lengths of cloth: black satin brocade for Sunday, gabardine for her man's suits, figured flannelette for underwear and little girls' dresses, bright prints for pillow slips, curtains, and bonnets, soft silk for neckerchiefs, dark sprigged goods for her vests, skirts, and jackets.

"The styles haven't changed in four hundred years," the man said. "If a woman's not hard on her clothes she can have an awful great many."

A colony spends about fifty thousand dollars a year (less than three hundred dollars per person) on things that are needed; nothing is spent on luxuries, which stimulate envy and greed. Smoking is sinful. One telephone serves the colony. Hutterites are not allowed to wear cosmetics or jewellery, not even wedding rings. They are not allowed to have cameras or pleasure cars to take their minds from the Lord. They are not allowed to have musical instruments.

"Our music must come from our hearts," I was told when the young people gathered in the evening at the tiny cabin provided for the provincial public-school teacher. "You do your own singing, not like in the world where everyone listens to somebody else on the radio," said Nadene Forsyth, the wise and captivating young teacher who came from "outside."

"I'm overfloated with happiness when I can listen to a radio," a young man said. "Last year the teacher had one and I came here every chance I got to learn old-time songs."

"I hat once a phonograph, just a liddle box it wass with 'Golden Slibbers' and 'Beaudiful Brown Eyes' and all dem nize records," a raffish young man told us. "I played it to myself in my room and one time I took it oud in the fields and played it for a couple of girls but my mother told the preajer on me and he made me sell it."

"Did he punish you?" Nadene asked.

"Yo, but he never punishes us bad, he just tells everybody in church what all sins we done and that shames us so we don't try it again for maybe a week anyways."

"It lasts longer than that," a sixteen-year-old said ruefully, and everyone laughed.

"He got caught sneaking out," they explained. "None of us are supposed to leave the colony without the preacher says so."

All talk and laughter were directed towards the teacher; everyone faced her with a smile of affection.

"Sing us a love song, Nadene," they begged.

"Teach it to us."

"Play us your saxophone, Nadene."

"The old folks don't like it," she said.

"They can't hear it this far from their houses, please play."

"I wish I could play dat ting," said a youngster.

"Th-Thing," corrected the teacher.

"I don't like being teached." The boy's blue eyes were teasing.

"You know you love going to school." Nadene's voice was cajoling.

"I like English school but not German school," the boy said. "The German teacher makes us learn two sides of the book for homework at nide and the next day we got to say it ride off and if we don't he gifs us a spanging on our behind with the willow, and that really hurts too, only I always learn mine so I don'd get it very ofden."

To learn Hutterite hymns, catechism, and history, printed only in German, the children go to German school in a room of the kindergarten building from seven to nine and from three-thirty to five every day; the time between is spent in regulation studies with the pretty public-school teacher.

"I'd love to go back to your school, Nadene," said Joe Wurtz, a young man with a lively brown face. "I'd like even to go to college already only they don't care much for education around here." He shrugged his broad shoulders and smiled happily. "We learn from experience: when we're fourteen we're through school and we go out in the pasture and pick ourself a team of colts to break, that makes us a man real quick."

At nine o'clock the girls in the group, who had sat shyly quiet all evening, said it was time to go home to bed.

I slept on a cot in the bedroom of two young women in one of the three rooms they shared with their aged parents and their older brother, Dave, who had a gentle face. Katie was little and dark. "She don't talk much but she thinks deep," I was told. Annie was older and jolly. "She went to Vulcan Colony yesterday to look for a hossband," Dave teased.

"And did she find one?" I asked.

"No." Annie laughed. "I'm too fat; these days they want them thin as a string bean."

When the rising bell rang at six-thirty the bearded father sang verse after verse of a German hymn in a voice that was strong and true.

"We like always to start the day singing," Dave told me when I went into the room where the old people sat, the father with a copy of *Ben Hur* on the table before him, the mother at the window quietly enduring the rheumatism that crippled her.

The bell called the adults to the dining hall for a breakfast of prunes, cheese, smoked ham, jam, bread, and coffee. The children ate together when the grownups had finished.

At seven-thirty the bell was rung again by one of the women and the two- to six-year-olds ran to the kindergarten where one of the older women supervised their play for the day.

In the communal kitchen, other women rolled dough into sheets thin as golden leaves; they laid the sheets over benches till each had done two or three, then, over their arms, the women carried the sheets of dough home and spread them on the counterpanes to dry before taking them back to the hall to be sliced into noodles.

The bell at ten-thirty meant that lunch was ready to be served to the little ones in the kindergarten. "Dat bell on de roof is a handy ting for keeping our women busy," a bearded patriarch told me.

The noon bell summoned us to dinner: the men sat on one side of the hall, the women on the other. On the shining, uncovered wooden tables were slices of crusty feather-light bread, pieces of celery, peeled beets, and individual graniteware plates. For every four people there were saucepans of boiled mutton and potatoes cooked in deep fat. Fingers were used more than forks, and gravy was sopped up from the communal dishes with bread.

The bell didn't ring again till four o'clock, when all the women walked sedately to the kitchen with their paring knives to peel potatoes for the next day.

It rang at five-thirty for the church service. As we watched the people going to the schoolhouse Dave told me, "We don't have to but we like to go to church every day to be reminded of how we should live. It keeps us in line. The preacher just came back from the funeral of a cousin in Montana so today he'll be telling how to prepare for death." Dave put his hand on his heart. "I haven't the words to express our belief in English," he said, "but I can feel it right here. I guess you'd say it was just trying to live the colony way without anger or envy, and loving one another – even those that condemn us for our peculiar ways."

The prayer meeting was over in half an hour. The men filed out of church, then the women, going straight to their supper of stewed duck giblets and necks; cabbage cooked to a mush with sugar; onions, buns, little balls of butter, and oval dishes of corn syrup. Everyone was enthusiastic about the duck but Joe Wurtz, who said it tasted like stinkweed.

Every evening I was invited to several homes in the colony. Though all had the same kind of furniture and were flawlessly clean and tidy, they had individuality: some had linoleum on the floor, some homemade mats; other had plants on the window sills, and some had sheepskins on the benches.

Wherever I visited the men did most of the talking. When they spoke of movies they had seen and other forbidden things they had done that made them seem men of the world, the women smiled quietly to themselves. Always wearing their kerchiefs on their heads, the mothers sat with their hands calmly clasped in their laps and listened with lively interest. They didn't wonder what their children were doing away from home. They had them always around them: the little ones knelt on the floor to pray and then were tucked into the sleep bench; round the lamp boys and girls studied their German lessons. The young men who had worked in the fields all day shaved and dressed up. Sometimes they called on the teacher or they walked with their girls in the lane beyond the caragana hedge; they came home early to sleep or sit on the benches around the room for conversation and singing.

The youngest son of Mike Wurtz, the carpenter, had taken his first steps on the day I called there. "You'd think by the time the sixth kid came along we'd be used to it, but it seems more wonderful to us than ever that our baby can walk," Mike said.

His wife took the child to her breast when he tired of his new-found prowess; Mike brought me an orange drink and a dish of sunflower seeds; his two little daughters, Dorothy and Magdalina, stared at me shyly then sat in turn on my knee. Benny brought me a toy to admire; Elizabeth, eleven, showed me the thread-counted cross-stitch sampler she was copying from one her mother had made when she was a little girl. Martha, the eldest, used the spinning wheel her father had made.

"Would you like us to sing for you?" Mike asked and he and his wife, with their children playing around them, sang "Among My Souvenirs" and a song about a girl named Tessie who left home and had a hard time. When they stopped we heard the preacher and his wife singing a hymn in their home on the other side of the wall.

As I walked through the colony to the next place where I was expected I heard singing in every house I passed.

A group of friends had gathered at the German schoolteacher's and they asked me many questions.

"Iss your hossband nice-looking?"

"Hass he got a blue suit?"

"What for do you need a whole house building for yourselfs?" They shook their heads in amazement.

"She has to have a kitchen and a room to eat," one told another.

"See, we got none of the bother," said Susie, who sat at the foot of the bed. "Only for one week in sixteen it is our turn to help with the cooking."

"We got five parties of eight to do the dishes," Annie told me.

"It's nice doing all things together, we never get lonesome," said Rachel.

The men were interested in hearing about airplane rides and

ships; they asked me about whales and different kinds of fish I had seen on the east coast.

"Have you ever seen mermaids?" the German teacher wondered.

"There ain't such things," Jake said.

"I don't believe in dem neither," said the teacher's wife. "They're just in stories for kits."

"Oh, yes, there's mermaids," said the teacher, and his large round eyes were solemn. "Christian Dornn seen one when he crossed over the ocean from Russia; he said it sang real nice."

All my evenings on the colony ended at the home of Jake Wurtz, the shepherd. The chests and benches around the room were always crowded with eager young people: the shepherd's almost grown-up family of six; Ike, Jake, and Smitty Wurtz, the preacher's sons; John Waldner, Dave Wurtz, and the sons of the boss, John and Joe Wipf, who had just come back to the colony from an unhappy sojourn in the world.

One evening we toasted marshmallows on the round stove that warmed the room. On another Joe showed me his water-colours and wood carvings, the seed plaques he'd made; he gave me a handkerchief on which he'd painted some flowers, and a pair of peach stones carved into baskets to keep my kerchief in place; he showed me his choicest possessions – a little ebony elephant and the plants he loved to raise. His mother demonstrated an ironing device that was used in olden times. Dan played his harmonica. Annie showed me her winter outfit: a plaid serge skirt and jacket.

"Our women don't have coats," Joe told me.

"They don't wear a lot of petticoats neither," another brother said.

Conversation was always enlivened with laughter or devoted to my instruction.

"We can't be baptized or married till we're ready to settle down and obey all our Hutterite laws," I was told. "Us boys are nearly twenty-five and we aren't baptized yet," Jake said, "but Annie is and she's only twenty-one."

"It's easier for the women: they never want to go to town and none of them ever left the colony yet," said John Wipf.

"They don't know no different, so they are always contented here," said Joe. "I am too," he added quickly, "but in winder there's not enough to do – we can just sit here and look out the window at the geese."

"We can read our Bible and our history books. There's some grand stories in there about our martyrs," Dave said.

"Yo, but you get sick of them."

"I like James Oliver Curwood," someone said.

"I like things that are true," said Dave. "I like awful well to read about our country; I think it is the grandest country in the world."

"It soon won't be our country if the Alberta government don't let us have more land."

And again I would be told what I had heard many times since I'd come to the colony: the great threat to the communal system that has so far given the Hutterites mental health and contentment.

The Old Elm, like most of the other Alberta colonies, is badly in need of expansion: the dining room is crowded, the schools are too small, there are no more rooms for newlyweds and growing families, there are too many men to be kept busy with the work of the farm, too many people to be supported by its produce (thirty Hutterites compared with 3.85 other Alberta farmers on a similar space). Normally, nearby land would be bought, new buildings put up, stock, equipment, and money of the old colony would be divided, and by lot it would be decided which families should move to the new site.

"But Alberta wants to be rid of us; they won't let us buy more land and we don't think that's fair." The preacher's son spoke with passion. "We pay our taxes, we don't get in trouble, we never go to courts, or mental hospitals, or to jail, we don't do no one any harm, we believe in letting other people live their own way the best that they can and we got to live the colony way or we're lost to the Lord."

"We got it preached to us that we are supposed to love our enemies and not get mad about what they do to us," Dave said quietly.

"It's hard to be friendly with people that show they despise us whenever we go into town," Ike said.

"They don't like us because we don't buy much from the fancy stores or give money for tobacco," said John Waldner.

"They were awful nasty to us during the war because our boys wouldn't fight and I guess we can't blame them but it is against our Hutterite religion and we can't help it," Ike said. "We done what we could, we went to work camps, our women done the men's work on the farm to grow food, we sent clothes to England and gave money for the Red Cross; now they say the veterans should have first choice of the land and we think that's only right – but the veterans aren't buying and they still won't let us."

"They want to chase us out to the wild woolies where there's nothing but coyotes and gopher holes," John said.

"They know we're good farmers and they want us to have poor land and make it good like we did here but they won't let us have enough to support a colony, only six sections and we need nine," Joe said. "We looked for land already in Saskatchewan and Mexico and Oregon and Montana but we don't want to leave Alberta. Most of us were born here and we love it on the prairies."

"We had before this to leave land that we loved," Dave said. "Our people from way back were chased around because they stuck to their faith. The last ones got chased out of Europe by Hitler and they found refuge in England."

"Well, I guess there's no use to worry. The Lord will take care of us like He always done."

"And that's for sure," said John.

On the day I left the colony Ike Wurtz drove me to town with a team of horses that shied every time a car speeded towards us on the highway. It took two and a half hours to drive the eleven miles to Magrath. Its main street was lined with cars, trucks, and shops, and its sidewalks were thronged with people: cowboys and schoolgirls bought tickets to go into the show; Indians smoked cigarettes around the door of the pool hall; children licked ice-cream cones in front of the drug store; somewhere a juke box was blaring; women carrying parcels rushed in and out of the stores.

The good-looking Hutterite boy who walked with dignity and confidence on his colony seemed to shrivel and slink along the busy street. The collarless homemade black suit that Ike wore to church with an air made him ill at ease and conspicuous. He heard people titter. He found it hard to smile and ignore their taunts as he had been taught to do; they made him feel ashamed and guilty of he knew not what.

As soon as he could, Ike finished his business in town, said goodbye to me, and turned Doll and Old Curly back towards the colony where he laughs as he helps the carpenter build a new chicken barn, is proud as he watches the erect, measured gait of the colony's women, the waddle of the fattening geese, the combines that cut through the grain of the colony's acres. And when the lamps are lit in the evening and his folks gather for conversation and singing he settles on a bench in the corner and enjoys the peace of his homely retreat from the bewildering world.

Maclean's, March 15, 1952

Twenty-five years after I stayed on the Old Elm Colony I called at Clear Springs, a new Hutterite settlement near Kenaston, Saskatchewan, where the Jacob Wurtz family was living. (It was their second move since they had left the Old Elm.) So unique are visitors to the colony that Dorothy Wurtz, who was eleven when I first met her, recognized me immediately when she saw me sitting at the wheel of my car. As soon as I got out I was surrounded by young and old women and children, greeting me joyously.

They showed me around the colony, proudly pointing out their new noodle-making machine, the milking machines, and the great machines that are used in the wheat fields.

Their long, low communal houses were more like apartments, having bedrooms, modern bathrooms, a small, barely furnished living room as well as a large basement for storage and recreation. They showed me someone's new baby. "Ain't he lovely?" an old woman said. "Not all babies turn out so good. One colony had five bad babies; they say it's the water causes it."

Joe Wurtz and his wife, Rebeccah, insisted that I stay with them. They brought food from the communal kitchen as a special treat in the evening when the young people gathered in their big basement room to ask questions and to listen. On the walls were glass-enclosed shelves displaying Indian arrowheads and artifacts, which Joe was excited about. "I'm the colony farm boss," he told me, "and I get the boys to look for these things when they're ploughing." Joe had the same enthusiasm and *joie de vivre* that he'd had as a boy of eighteen.

I asked him if he was still painting flowers on handkerchiefs. He laughed and said, "No, but we'd like to paint our bedroom a nice peach colour, only we mayn't because everybody else would want the same and that would cost too much paint."

When I asked if he and Rebeccah could ever come to visit me, he said, "Oh no, they'd never let us do that because everybody else couldn't go too."

He looked over the colony's broad, waving wheat fields. "Besides, though we'd sure like to come to see you, Edna, we don't really care that much to go to Ontario; they say the land is mostly just scrub."

Those Mouth-Watering Mennonite Meals

Whon Ian Sclanders, articles editor of
Maclean's, asked me to write about the
fabulous food of my Old Order Mennonite friends, I
found the research was the most enjoyable of any
I've ever done.

Almost every Friday throughout the fall and winter
of 1953-54 I drove to Bevvy Martin's farmhouse to
talk about food and to watch her prepare it. For every
dinner and supper she made something different.
While she hovered over the stove or mixing bowl, I
drooled and copied her recipes. Then I sat with the
family to eat myself full of *drepsley* soup, *schnippled*
bean salad, summer sausage, *fetschpatze* (fat
sparrows), *schnitz* and shoofly pie, or dozens of other
delectables that I've since tried to immortalize.

O ne of the joys of my life is to visit my Mennonite friends the Martins in their sprawling old fieldstone farmhouse near the Conestoga River in Waterloo County, Ontario. Their large, old-fashioned kitchen, warmed by a big black cook-stove, always has a homely fragrance of wonderful things to eat. Sometimes there is an apple smell, sometimes an aroma of *rivel* soup, roasting meat, baking cinnamon buns or spicy *botzelbawm* pie.

Bevvy, the plump little lady of the house, is always busy *schnitzing* (slicing), canning, or cooking. The wings of her soft brown hair are smoothly parted under her organdie prayer cap, and she wears a plain navy-blue dress with a skirt almost down to her ankles. She greets me with a smile and a hand-shake: "Of course you'll stay for supper," she says as she hangs up my coat on a nail. "You know we feel real bad if you come for a wisit and don't make out a meal."

I readily accept, always and often – resigning my figure to limbo.

The food Bevvy cooks has such mouth-watering savour that no one can resist it. Like all Mennonite cooking it is plain but divinely flavoured and different from any other. You don't have to belong to the Mennonite faith to enjoy it: everyone who has grown up in Waterloo County, where Pennsylvania Dutch Mennonites settled in 1797, is devoted to sour-cream salads and the richness of Dutch apple pie. Visitors and newcomers beg for recipes that have passed from generation to generation of Mennonite housewives without being printed in a cookbook. Everyone who tastes *schnitz und knepp*, crusty golden *ponhaus* and luscious shoofly pie wants to know how to prepare them.

Economy and experience are the keynotes of Mennonite cooking. Recipes are invented to make use of everything that is grown on Waterloo County farms. Fruits are canned and pickled and made into juicy pies. Beef and ham are cured with maple smoke; pork scraps become well-seasoned sausages. Sour milk is made into cheeses; sour cream is used in fat cakes and in salads. Stale bread is crumbled and browned with butter to give zest to vegetables, noodles, and dumplings. Nothing is ever wasted and every meal is a feast.

"Today it gives *drepsley* soup, dandelion salad, and *fet-*

schpatze [fat sparrows]," Bevvy tells me as she puts on a clean print apron, tying it first in front to be sure the bow is even, then pulling it round and patting it over her stomach. I sit in the rocker by the kitchen window while she bustles between the sink, the stove, and the big, square table covered with a bright-figured oilcloth. "You don't mind if I keep on working while we wisit," she says. "The curds are getting that smell I don't like round the house and I have to quick make my *haafe kase* [crock cheese]."

She melts butter in a graniteware kettle and into it pours sour-milk curds that have been scalded, crumbled, and ripened for three or four days. She stirs the mass till it melts to the colour of honey, adds cream, and keeps stirring till it comes to a boil that goes *poof!* then pours it into a crock and sets it away in the pantry. "Do you want to lick the dish?" She gives me a spoon and the kettle to scrape. "Some like it better with caraway seed in but we rather have it chust plain." Sampling its mild, mellow goodness, I agree that it couldn't be better.

As she works at the kitchen sink Bevvy glances through the window above it. "I look up the lane every once in a while to see if there's a horse and rig coming for supper," she says. "We love to have company drop in."

"Does it happen often?"

"Not so much during the week, but every Sunday when we have service in the church nearest us people come here for dinner. Sometimes there's not so many, maybe chust a family or two, but sometimes we might have thirty-five. We never know, they chust come."

"Without being specially invited?"

"Ach, our people are always welcome. They know we have plenty to eat and it don't take long to get ready when everyone helps. Come once and I'll show you."

In a dark pantry off the kitchen she shows me crocks of cheese, elderberries, *latwaerrich* (apple butter), bags full of *schnitz*, dried corn and beans, pails of maple syrup, honey, and sacks of sugar and flour.

The cellar looks like a store. A room twelve feet square has shelves all round it from the floor to the ceiling filled with quart and half-gallon jars of fruit, vegetables, jam, and pickled things. On a larder that hangs from the ceiling in the centre of the room are pies and buns and cakes. On the floor there are crocks of head cheese, jars of canned beef and chicken, and pork sausage sealed with lard.

In another room smoked meats and sausages hang from the beams above us. There are great bins of potatoes and turnips. Other vegetables are stored in boxes of leaves and there are barrels full of apples.

"This is our work for the summer and fall," Bevvy says. "We like work and it makes us feel good when we have it away in the cellar."

When Bevvy's children come from school and their chores in the barn are all done, Amsey, aged ten, the very shy youngest, in black stovepipe pants and a collarless jacket, shines up a basket of apples, then happily makes a bowlful of popcorn because there is company to treat.

Bevvy's merry, pretty daughter Lyddy Ann, who is thirteen and dressed like her mother except that she has pigtails and doesn't wear a cap, sets the kitchen table with ironstone china and the staples that are on it for breakfast, dinner, and supper. There is bread, butter, and jam: "We were taught we'd be sick if we didn't eat jam-bread at the front part of every meal," Bevvy says. There are pickles and dishes of sours: "We may never leave anything on our plates and sometimes a little relish on a piece of *schpeck* [fat meat] helps to make it swallow," Lyddy says. For every meal there are potatoes and coffee.

At least twice a day there's a plateful of summer sausage. For breakfast there is, in addition, coffee cake, porridge or cornmeal mush, and a bowlful of *schnitz* and *gwetcha* (dried apples and prunes cooked together). For dinner and supper there is always a bowl of fruit, a plateful of cookies or cake, pudding, and pie – besides soup and the main course. When I tease Bevvy about having three desserts she says, "Canned peaches are not dessert, they are chust fruit. Pudding is not dessert neither, it is only for filling the corners, and cookies and pie are chust natural for anybody to have."

On the stove there's a kettle of simmering beef broth; a pot of potatoes is boiling; ham is frying in an iron pan; a sauce for the salad is thickening; and in a pan of hot lard the *fetschpatze* are becoming a tender golden brown.

Bevvy's great, handsome husband, David, wearing a plaid shirt and overalls, and her seventeen-year-old Salome, dressed like Lyddy Ann, come in from their work in the barn. They greet me with hearty handshakes, then wash themselves and comb their hair at the sink.

At the stove there's a clatter of action. Bevvy puts the baked *fetschpatze* into the warming closet with the meat and potatoes. Into the beef broth she lets drop through a colander a batter of egg, milk, and flour. Lyddy mixes the salad. Bevvy adds parsley to the soup and pours it into a bowl.

We sit around the bountiful table and bow our heads in a long silent prayer.

Everyone reaches for a piece of bread. The steaming soup bowl is passed among us and we ladle onto our dinner plates its clear fragrant broth thickened by tiny dumplings. Bevvy says, "Grossmommy Brubacher always told us *drepsley* [dripped batter] soup is especially nourishing for the sick."

"But I ain't sick." David's bright brown eyes are teasing. "I guess that's why I rather always would have bean soup."

"Ach, you like any thick soup where I sprinkle buttered browned bread crumbs on," Bevvy says with a smug little smile.

"Except *rivel* soup," Amsey reminds her. It is made from milk thickened with egg and flour rubbed into *rivels* (crumbs), Lyddy tells me.

"He eats that too if he has a slice of raw onion and summer sausage with," Bevvy says.

"Ach, I eat anything if I like it real good or not, that's how we are taught not to waste." David holds his spoon like a sceptre.

"Have you never tried canned soup?" I ask him.

"We never bought a can of anything yet," Bevvy answers. "We always chust make our own."

"We got more different kinds yet than they got in the stores," Salome says. "We make soup from our vegetables, from our meat, from our leftovers, and we have all kinds of milk soups. I think we make soup out of everything you could put in your mouth to eat."

"Ach, Salome, that ain't right." Amsey looks at his sister reproachfully. "You know we never yet had soup made from huckleberry pie." He sopped up the remains of his *drepsley* soup with buttered bread to clean his plate for *kochkase*, summer sausage, pickled beets, and salad.

Sour cream and vinegar is the dressing for most Pennsylvania Dutch Mennonite salads. With finely grated onion it is poured over lettuce or spinach leaves, cucumbers, boiled *schnippled* string beans, and hot or cold chopped cabbage.

Dandelion salad can be made only in springtime when the greens are pale and tender. In autumn Bevvy mixes curly yellow-leaved endive with the same piquant sauce which can also be used to make hot potato salad. She fries bits of bacon in a pan till they're crisp then takes them out and stirs a little flour into the fat. She beats an egg or two in a bowl, adds sour cream, salt, pepper, and vinegar, then carefully pours the mixture into the pan and stirs till it's fairly thick. When it is slightly cooled she mixes it with the dandelion and garnishes it with hard-boiled eggs and the bacon bits.

As we eat it with smoked ham and mashed potatoes Bevvy says, "The salad we like the best, and easy to make for whatever crisp greens you have, is a real old-time recipe I got from David's mother. For each person to be served, you fry a slice of bacon till it crackles, take it out and to the fat in the pan put one teaspoon of brown sugar, one teaspoon vinegar and some salt and pepper; it will sizzle and spit so have care for yourself. And the sugar might get kind of lumpy. Let it melt again, then cool it all a little before you mix in two tablespoonfuls of sour cream. Now pour it over the greens and the bacon broken in with it and on top slice tomato or radish rings or anything nice-looking you got that goes good."

"Then put it quick on the table and it will soon be all," Lyddy adds.

"I never seen you measure it that way yet," Salome says to her mother.

"Ach, I made it so often already I chust put in what I think. Like for most things, I tell by the feel or the taste. The way we cook got handed down from cheneration to cheneration. Since I was a little girl I helped my mam and I learned from her chust like my girls learn from me. That's why it's hard to give exact amounts of a recipe to a stranger."

Lyddy says, "She tells us, 'Put in a little handful of this, or a big handful of that, a pinch of one thing or half-an-eggshell of something else, or a lump the size of a butternut.' It's always 'Flour to stiffen or enough to make a thin batter.' And for soup and the like of that it's 'Put in milk or water up to the second scratch in the kettle!'"

Bevvy laughs. "Ach, well, so it must be. How much you make depends on how many people you cook for. We don't like to run short on anything but we don't like to waste nothing neither."

"She usually guesses chust right," Amsey says, "except when it's brown-sugar sauce for the apple dumplings and I could eat extra."

Bevvy cooks all her meats and vegetables without consulting a guide and their flavour is magnificent. She makes potpies of pigeons and rabbits and veal. She roasts beef, pork, and lamb. Her gravies are brown and shiny. She fries chickens in butter and, dipped in egg and bread crumbs, the little fish that Amsey catches in the river. She cooks sauerkraut with succulent spareribs. In an iron pot she makes stew and pot roasts browned with onions and bay leaves. Sometimes she has duck or roast goose bursting with savoury dressing.

"But we don't always have fresh meat in the country," Bevvy says. "Only right after we butcher. We have to cure it to keep it. Some we make into sausage, some we pack solid in jars and steam it, we smoke beef and ham. What we like best is the summer sausage: it is beef and pork ground real fine with seasoning and saltpetre, then stuffed tight in cotton bags the size of a lady's stocking and smoked for a week with maple smoke."

"We can eat that every day, we never get sick of it," David says.

"We couldn't live without summer sausage," little Amsey says as he slaps a slice on a piece of bread and butter.

"Ach, we could live without only we rather wouldn't," Bevvy says. "We got all other kinds yet, like *schwaudamawge* sausage and liverwurst and head cheese: they're mostly made from the pork scraps but they go good with fried potatoes and pickled small corn on the cob or beet and red-cabbage salad."

Salome says, "I rather have *schnitz und knepp* [dried apples boiled with a ham bone and dumplings]."

"Me too," says Lyddy Ann.

"You should see these women," David says, "how they sit sometimes all day *schnitzing* apples and drying them for the winter. Or making *latwaerrich* from cider and apples and cinnamon boiled and stirred half a day till it is red-brown and thick enough to spread with *schmier kase* on bread." He licks his lips and shakes his head. "Oh my, but that is good."

"She'll think we're a pig the way we make so much of our food," Lyddy says.

Bevvy smiles at me calmly. "She knows we work hard and we need it and never throw anything away."

Not even a piece of bread. Before it's too stale Bevvy uses it for pudding or stuffing in tenderloin, spareribs, or fowl. She breaks pieces of bread into milk soups. When it is hard as a cracker she grinds it and keeps it in jars to mix with cheese on a casserole dish or to brown with butter and sprinkle over cooked vegetables, brown buttered dumplings, with onions, and anything made with a cream sauce.

"One of our strictest rules is never to waste a thing," Bevvy says. "When the Mennonites were over in Switzerland yet they got chased around by those that didn't like their peace-loving religion and I guess they had to eat whatever they could get. Then in 1683 they started coming to Pennsylvania and gradually had things a little easier. But those that came up here to Ontario after the American Revolution were pretty poor again. Even if they had money they couldn't buy anything yet because there was nothing here but bush till they cleared the land and started to grow things.

"It's only lately since I grew up that we bought food in the stores except sugar and spices and salt. We only used what we grew in our own fields and garden and made recipes up to suit."

From a drawer in the cupboard Bevvy brings me her most treasured possession: a little handwritten black notebook in which she has copied recipes of special things to bake or pickle or can. It is well worn and some of its pages are spattered with butter or batter. At the top of each page is written the name of the recipe's donor. There is Aunt Magadaline's Hurry Cake, Grossmommy Martin's *Kuddlefleck* and Cantaloupe Pickle, Salome Gingerich's Ground Cherry Preserve. "When I see those names," Bevvy says, "I know chust how it tasted because most of the recipes I got when I ate at their places."

This is Cousin Lydia's recipe for *fetschpatze* ("fat sparrows" because of the odd shapes they take when spoonfuls of batter are dropped in hot lard):

> 1 beaten egg
> a little salt
> 1 cup sour cream or sour milk
> 1 round teaspoon of soda
> flour to stiffen

"We eat them hot and dunked in maple syrup," Bevvy says as they are passed around the table. And we all eat so many that David says, "It wonders me that we'll have room after this for the pie. But we will."

Pie appears on Bevvy's table three times a day. Every Friday she and Salome bake twenty pies and store them away in the cellar. If company comes on Sunday after divine service the pies may all be used at once; if not, there'll be enough pies to last the week. Their variety is infinite: besides all the fruit, milk, and mince pies there are sour-cream raisin, tomato, cottage cheese, buttermilk, *botzelbawm* (somersault), and some invented on the spur of the moment to keep things from being wasted.

Dutch apple, or *schnitz*, has various versions. Sometimes Bevvy makes hers extra rich: she places the *schnitz* (segments of apple) close together in a pie shell then dabs over every piece a mixture of melted butter, brown sugar, and cornstarch. With crumbs of flour, brown sugar, and butter she fills up the spaces and covers the apples, then dribbles a few spoonfuls of sour cream on top and sprinkles the pie with cinnamon. After it's baked and cooled you wish you could smell it and eat it forever.

Shoofly pie no doubt got its name because it tempts more than just people. Bevvy says it's a Mennonite favourite because it keeps well in a cellar. Her recipe calls for equal parts of baking molasses and water and a pinch of soda poured into an unbaked shell and covered with crumbs made of flour, brown sugar, and butter. Sometimes she makes it with maple syrup and calls it candy pie. Then it's so gooey and luscious that it is ravished before it can reach the cellar.

When I ask Amsey which is his favourite, he says, "Peach pie made with the peelings."

Bevvy smiles apologetically. "We make it sometimes with

the peelings after we did the canning. We chust boil them with sugar and a little water till it's almost like jam then we put it in a baked pie shell and cover it with whipped cream or boiled custard."

Amsey rolls his big brown eyes. "And that really *schmecks* [tastes]!"

Every plate on the Martins' table is as clean as if it had not been used when we finish eating our supper. David sits back in his chair with a grunt of great satisfaction and dexterously uses a toothpick. Lyddy glances at me and laughs. "You look like you have afraid you'll bust your buttons."

"I am; I think I've gained five pounds since I sat down."

"Ach, not chust from one meal," Bevvy says.

David's eyes have a twinkle. "If she eats with us for a week she'll be wonderful fat."

"Like Aunt Hannah," says Amsey.

"Shame on youse," Bevvy chides, "she ain't got the frame to sit that broad."

"I'd certainly lose my waistline if I ate much of your wonderful cooking."

David grins and pats his well-rounded belly. "I'm glad our people ain't so stylish that they care about getting fat. We chust eat ourselves till we're full."

Maclean's, April 1, 1954

Bevvy Martin is eighty years old now and no longer prepares three feasts a day. She and David tend their large garden, eat very well, but watch their weight and their diet – until visitors drop in: then David gets a container of ice cream from the freezer and Bevvy cuts up a pie or a cake she has just taken out of the oven.

Since eating so many great meals in Bevvy's kitchen I have been swapping and inventing recipes, trying to cook in the old-fashioned Mennonite way. When friends come to eat with me I might give them *drepsley* soup, sour cream salads, farmer's sausage, and *schnitz* or *botzelbawm* pie.

"Why don't you write a cookbook with these fabulous recipes?" my guests used to ask me and I'd tell them I'd like to, but who would publish it?

Then one day in 1966 a letter came from Ryerson Press asking if I'd write a book on Mennonite-country cooking. I answered immediately that I'd certainly try.

Bevvy loaned me her little hand-written black recipe book; I kept calling my mother to find out how she made things that had brought bliss to my childhood; I put down recipes from my sisters', my neighbours', my friends', and my own collections. Two years later I had tested and recorded more than seven hundred recipes that were soon published in *Food That Really Schmecks* (now with McGraw-Hill Ryerson).

Because thousands of readers and several publishers kept begging for a sequel, *More Food That Really Schmecks* was published in 1979 (by McClelland and Stewart).

"When can we expect *Still More Food That Really Schmecks?*" people and publishers ask me. I don't know. It may be on its way; I never stop trying new recipes. Writing cookbooks is rather like stamp collecting. There is never an end. And I do love to eat.

◆

The Unconquered Warriors
of the Six Nations

*I*n 1955 *Maclean's* asked me to go to the Six
Nations Indian Reserve near Brantford, Ontario, to
see what the Iroquois now think about Joseph Brant,
the war chief who led their people to Canada after
they'd fought with the British in the American War
of Independence. I soon found out that Brant was not
the popular Indian hero the white man revered.

The Iroquois never did submit to the white man;
they consider themselves allies, not subjects of the
British – and they still won't give in. Many won't
take an oath of allegiance to Canada; many won't
vote in Canadian elections; hundreds cling to the
ancient Longhouse religion.

I came home with one hundred sixty pages of
notes about these friendly imaginative people in their
unrecognized "independent republic" in the heart of
Ontario.

Old Bob Henhawk was sitting on a log behind his unpainted little frame house, smoking his pipe. Hanging from the trees along the path to his frog pond were his scythe, a bucket without a bottom, some horseshoes, cow horns, coils of rusty wire, and a rake. A breeze fluffed out the long grey hair that hung under his well-seasoned hat. His strong red-brown face was turned towards the rough gravel road that led into the Indian reserve from the smooth busy highway to Brantford, Ontario, eight miles away.

"I hear they got some pretty good roads out there among the whites," he told me as a passing car raised the dust. "Next thing they'll be paving in here." He drew on his pipe reflectively. "Never needed to pave in the old days; never had dust. Indian trails through the bush were narrow and clean." He took his pipe from his mouth and leaned over to pull a fattening wood tick from the chest of his mongrel dog, Nosey. "White fellow come in here one day and said to me, 'Ain't you glad we civilized you? You got much more now than you had.'" He straightened his slender old shoulders. "I says to him, 'The whites never beat us in a war but seems now like they think they bought us. All we want is our freedom.'"

Old Bob Henhawk is a chief of the Iroquois, who not long ago were naked, whooping savages – the history books say – burning, torturing, scalping, and eating the flesh of their victims. They comprised the democratic League of Six Nations – Mohawks, Cayugas, Onondagas, Oneidas, Tuscaroras, Senecas – who lived together in peace and supported one another in war for more than four hundred years. They called themselves Men of Men, terrorized the French settlers in Canada, and were supreme over all other Indians east of the Mississippi, from Georgian Bay to Florida.

Now their council fires have been stamped out. Their Longhouses of cedar bark have gone down. (The Longhouse is a place of feasting and dancing for those who still worship their Creator in the Indian way.) English has become the common tongue of the Six Nations, whose six languages are as different from one another as German, French, and Chinese. The white man has confined the proud Iroquois to reservations, small tracts of land set aside for their exclusive use in Ontario, Quebec, and New York.

The reserve Chief Henhawk lives on with six thousand of his people is a plot of dismal farmland about twelve miles square beside the Grand River in southern Ontario. It is a small part of the tract gratefully given in 1784 by George III of England to the followers of Joseph Brant, the Iroquois war chief who led his people into the War of American Independence to fight for the British. The grant was made as a recompense for the lands in the northeastern states that had belonged, from time immemorial, to the League of Six Nations and that Britain had ceded to the victorious Americans.

Soon after the Iroquois moved to the tract they had earned with their blood and their sacrifice, white settlers and land speculators from America and Britain came and encroached on the land. Some paid for their acres; some had land given to them by Joseph Brant; others just squatted. The country was flooded with illegal deeds but the courts upheld the white men and ignored the rights of the Indians, who had no individual titles to property. When the Indians protested, Upper Canada in 1835 segregated them from the white men by forcing them to sell and surrender, for little more than eight hundred thousand dollars, all their grant except the timberless acres of what is now the reservation. This money is still held for them in trust by the federal government, with the interest being spent as the Indian Affairs branch decides. Canada administers the Iroquois reserve the same way it administers all other Indian reservations in the country, forgetting that the Six Nations have a treaty with Britain, which calls them her allies, not subjects.

Canada considers the Six Nations tract Crown land: no one living on it can get a clear title to property or borrow money to build or buy. The Indians are exempt from paying property taxes but the interest on their own trust fund, they say, should be enough to keep up their roads, schools, hospital, and other public services. Money earned on the reserve is exempt from income tax, but only school teachers and a very few others can make enough there to benefit from the exemption; two thirds of the Indians commute to work in nearby cities and farms and have to pay tax on their incomes, which are earned off the reserve. They pay all other taxes that Canadians pay.

Canada has tricked them and robbed them and broken their

treaties, the Iroquois say. They claim Canada has no right to govern them at all and that their land is not a reservation but a sovereign state in North America, as Switzerland is a country in Europe. They write their own passports, which are honoured abroad.

The unconquered Iroquois refuse to take oaths of allegiance to any land except the confederacy of the Six Nations. Their loyalty is unswerving. Even though some have lived and worked for many years in faraway cities, they call the Six Nations country their home and insist on being enumerated there when a census is taken.

Clinging to their past independence, old men like Chief Henhawk dream of the days when their fathers wandered free in the forest, where they hunted and fished while their wives hoed the corn. While most of those who work off the reserve buy cars and TV sets, can't speak their tribal languages, and can't speed a snowsnake or swing a lacrosse stick, they brood on their glorious heritage. The ones who stay home on their poor little farms lament and protest and hope and stop hoping that they'll prove they are still a great nation. One Iroquois, who is realistic and prosperous, told me the sooner they become Canadians and have to give up the reserve the better it will be for all of them.

But the hereditary chiefs advise them not to accept the doubtful new privilege of voting in Ontario's elections; it might lead to Canadian citizenship, land tax, and the loss of their homes. They dread their absorption by the white man. Canada, they say, is a foreign power that threatens extermination of their proud race.

They send delegations to Ottawa to protest interference. They appeal to the courts as the white man keeps filching more of their land. They have presented their grievances to the League of Nations at Geneva, the San Francisco Conference, and the United Nations Assembly, asking that they be freed from the dictatorship of Canada's Indian Act, which makes them wards of the government. They want complete freedom – their own laws, their own lands, their own money.

A treaty with the British crown gives them a status different from that of other Indians in Canada. At the end of the War of American Independence, in which they fought valiantly for the British, they were dispossessed of their villages and their beautiful lake-spangled hunting grounds in Pennsylvania, New York, and Ohio. To compensate them for their losses, Britain gave to her "faithful allies" the lands of the Grand River Valley, six miles deep on each side of the stream from its mouth, at Lake Erie, to the source, one hundred eighty miles inland, "for them and their posterity to enjoy forever."

At the time of the grant, 1784, the Grand flowed through wilderness that no white man wanted. Now the fertile valley has four flourishing cities – Kitchener, Waterloo, Galt, and Brantford – forty-odd towns and villages, some of the richest farms in Ontario, and almost four hundred thousand white people. The lands of the Iroquois have shrunk to a plot of hard clay marshland, scrub bush, a muddy creek too shallow to float a canoe, and a ten-mile frontage on one side of the Grand River.

The Six Nations Reserve is a flat, dejected little island land-locked by lush hills and the bustle of industrial plenty. At its borders all paved highways end abruptly. "That's how you know you are there," people say. The roads that divide it into one-and-a-half-mile squares are rough gravel or deeply rutted clay. The farms look less productive than those on the outside; barns are smaller and shabbier; there are fewer cattle and tractors; many fields are untended. About a quarter of a mile apart, or gathered together at the corners where they catch all the dust from the roads, are old one-room log houses, tar-paper shacks with a clutter of things around them, many neat little homes covered with asbestos shingle, and some fair-sized brick houses or new ranch-style homes of painted clapboard. Scattered widely are garages and stores, fifteen grade-schools, several brick churches, small stucco missions, and four Long-houses of faded frame.

On a crossroads near the centre of the reservation is the village of Ohsweken, the capital of the Six Nations country. There its parliament meets in the council house, a small, white-brick building that looks like an old township hall; on its broad, shady lawn a memorial honours the hundreds of Iroquois braves who fought in two world wars as Canadians. There is a government-subsidized hospital, a co-operative agricultural building, an Orange Lodge hall, and a funeral parlour. There is a new school equipped to teach home economics and industrial arts, the gift of Canada's government, and a smaller grade-school built by Six Nations funds. There are a few stores and houses, two churches and manses, the greatly resented quarters of the RCMP, and a friendly little restaurant with a bulletin board that announces when there is a bingo in Buffalo, New York, with bottles of whisky for prizes.

Ohsweken looks not unlike any sleepy Canadian hamlet, except that most of the people who come there from all over the reservation have black hair, dark eyes, and high cheekbones, small hands, small feet, and skin that is swarthier than just a good tan. They dress like any rural Canadians. Their names might be Canadian: Hill, Green, Martin, Freeman, Jamieson, Anderson, Sky. They are Anglican, United Church, Baptist; there are no Roman Catholics, and only a smattering of Adventists or Mormons. And there are twelve hundred who belong to the Longhouse but celebrate Christmas with gifts and a tree.

While I was visiting the reservation I boarded at the home of William Johnson, a Mohawk and Anglican, a veteran of the First World War. He had a big garden out front and did odd jobs in the village. Mrs. Johnson made good rhubarb pie and fried pork chops and sighed about her weight. Their house, spotlessly clean and well-furnished, had electrical equipment but no running water.

Every day I was there I called on people in all parts of the Six Nations country. Though I was white and intruding with questions about Iroquois ways, I was always cordially welcomed. If I came close to a mealtime the housewife put a plate on the table for me. "That's how Iroquois does," Chief Henhawk told me. "It is educated right into our children that girl, no matter if she's a stranger, she's your sister, and all old women is your mother, and same way with the men. Tecumseh dropped the poor Delawares here in 1813 and they ain't left us yet, and when the Mississaugas sold their land at Port Credit they asked shelter here for a day and a night; now they got five squares of our land." The chief shrugged his shoulders. "We can't put 'em out, they're our brothers."

I went often to call on Chief Henhawk. We sat in his

scraggly woodlot near the outbuildings that were little more than boards leaning against one another. I sat on a chair he brought from his house and he sat on one he told me his daddy had made before he was born.

"I think the real old Indians must have been pretty nice people," he said as he reached for a wood tick that had got down the back of his shirt. "They had not one blaspheming word in their language." He cracked the insect between his fingernails, then drew peacefully again on his pipe. "Way back, maybe a million years ago, all the leaders got together and they looked at the stars and the moon and the sun going round, and the rains came and they got the benefit of it and they thought there must be something makes things so good and they got the idea of a Creator. They knew the Creator of good things must be good and they figured people should be good like that too. They never forgot it and they teached their young ones, and they teached theirs when they come along, and that's how it was carried on through the years. Nothing wrote down. We just have to look around us to see it." His eyes swept his bit of woodlot, his small shallow pond, and the sky.

He looked at me, shaking his shaggy old head. "But the whites keep trying to change it," he said. "I was talking one day to a preacher. Asked me why I didn't give up being pagan. He said it was a sin the way the Indians dance and feast at the Longhouse.

"I said to him, 'Now you got three children and sometimes you go into town. Perhaps some day you say, 'Now this time I'm going to bring you all presents. I'll bring this one a doll and that one a gun and the other some candy.' All day the children wait for you to come home and at four o'clock, say, you come and you give what you bought 'em." Chief Henhawk stood up, put his hands in the air, and danced up and down. "You see," he said, smiling, "the children are glad and they dance for joy and thanksgiving. I said to the preacher, 'Are your children pagans?'"

All the Iroquois feasts are feasts of thanksgiving, Chief Henhawk told me. They give thanks for everything that grows in the woods and the fields. The biggest feast of the year, lasting five or six days, comes when the back of the winter is broken; then there is the feast of the maple sap, the planting of seed, the wild strawberry feast, feasts for peas, beans, green corn, and pumpkins. "The chiefs start a feast by telling the people how to be good," he explained. "They haven't got the words 'Don't do this, don't do that' to give people bad ideas. They just got the words for goodness."

I called one day on Mrs. Alma Green, who lived near Chief Henhawk in a house with a blue roof and a lean-to that sheltered her shiny red car. She told me any white person who stayed in the Six Nations country without permission of the council was a trespasser. She was a thin, grey-haired woman who had once been a teacher, a lumber-camp cook, a church organist, a reporter for the *Toronto Star*, and had six times gone to Ottawa to talk to men of high rank about the plight of her Indian people. She now commutes every day to Brantford, where she punches a factory time clock.

In her living room there was a TV set, a cabinet full of china figurines, five cats, each asleep on a cushioned chair, a picture of long-skirted fair ladies in front of a castle and, on the wall above the sofa where she sat, a copy of the Lord's prayer carved in wood.

"I am bitter," she told me. "If I went outside this minute and saw your car and got into it and drove away because I had discovered it, would that make it mine?" Her dark eyes narrowed angrily. "That's how the white man got our lands. We trusted him and he cheated us."

She went out of the room to fetch a leather briefcase and showed me copies of treaties the British had broken, letters that proved Iroquois lands had been stolen, and emblazoned on buckskin, the wording of the treaty that gave the Six Nations the Grand River Valley.

"Do you blame us for being mistrustful?" she asked. Then she told me that Canada, not content with depriving them of their lands, in 1924 had disbanded the council of hereditary chiefs that had guarded the interests of the confederacy for more than four hundred years, and forced an elective system on the reserve. Twelve councilors and a chief councilor now seek election, like the aldermen and mayor of a town. They meet regularly with the Indian agent at Ohsweken to administer the internal affairs of the reserve. "But they don't represent our people," Mrs. Green said. "Not ten per cent vote; no Iroquois who is loyal to the Six Nations would vote for a man who must swear allegiance to the crown when he is elected." She chased a cat that jumped up on the sofa beside her. "Occasionally a good, intelligent Indian goes into the council, but he isn't given a chance. If he tries to do anything to better our ways he's told to sit down and keep quiet or get out. He has to obey the Indian agent who gets his orders from Ottawa." Mrs. Green frowned. "But our hereditary chiefs still meet in the Longhouses; they fight for our rights and tell us what to do."

Mrs. Green put her papers back into her briefcase. "Of course I blame many injustices on Joseph Brant, our own leader. He was the only Iroquois in his time who could speak English, so he was appointed to deal with the British. They treated him like a king. He made decisions without consulting the chiefs, he led us into war, he brought us up here and, flattered by the white man, gave away lands that were not his to give. The white men called him a hero – you have seen his bronze statue in Brantford. He was noble in everything he did. But he betrayed his own people. And for that I could kick him in the pants." Her foot jerked involuntarily.

"Brant was a Mohawk but he never learned the religion of his tribe. He was brought up by an Anglican minister and took Christianity so seriously that the British used him to convert his people. They listened to the missionaries and slid away from the Longhouse." Her intense dark eyes stared straight ahead as she spoke. "Our forefathers prophesied that if we stepped into the white man's canoe desolation would befall us," she said solemnly. "That has come to pass. The Mohawk has no Longhouse now. Christianity has brought only sorrow. We are a lost people.

"Sometimes I go to the Longhouses of the Onondagas, the Cayugas, or the Senecas," Mrs. Green went on. "I don't need a new dress or new hat to go there. The people are humble and penitent; the old ones, so sincere, have no stain of sin. But I don't understand their language. I don't feel at home among them." She held up her hands and looked from one to the other. "I am always between two fences."

One sunny, warm morning I drove past the Onondaga Longhouse, a plain, low-gabled frame building with small-paned windows and not enough paint. Its only door was open and I stopped to look in. Two rows of benches stood round pumpkin-yellow walls. At each end of the room was a round-bellied stove, and between them two long, backless benches stood end to end with an oil lamp hanging above. A man was sweeping the unstained pine floor. He wore a red headband with a single feather, a factory-made fringed buckskin jacket, coloured beads around his neck, dark trousers with long black hair from a horse's mane sewn into the side seams, a beaded belt, and a handsomely decorated apron that hung front and back.

"Come in, come in," he called when he saw me. "We're having a dance here today. You're welcome to stay if you want to." He paused in his sweeping. "Not a worldly dance; it's a feast to give thanks for the sun and the moon and seed to be planted."

He said the ceremony would begin at eleven o'clock, but no one arrived till past noon. Most people came in their cars. They spoke to each other in the Onondaga language. The men wore plaid shirts or jerseys, dark trousers or jeans, the women their best rayon dresses; two little boys had headdresses of feathers bought in the fifteen-cent store. A woman with a permanent explained to me that not many have Indian costumes to wear any more; they can't get the buckskins and feathers of eagles.

At one-thirty we went into the Longhouse. All the women and little children sat at one end, the men and boys at the other. The man who had been sweeping the floor was standing at the men's end preaching in dialect, his tones impassioned, pleading, or monotonous. When he sat four other chiefs rose in turn, gave a high whooping call, chanted as they walked five paces forward and back to their benches.

During the hour that the preaching went on, more people wandered into the Longhouse till there must have been more than a hundred. Little children kept getting drinks of water from a dipper in a pail. Two large butcher's baskets covered with paper were brought in and put on the floor near the stove at the women's end of the room. Then a great iron kettle full of steaming grey corn soup, thick as library paste, was set down beside it.

The youngest chief dusted off one of the benches in the centre of the room and two men sat down facing each other. One shook a rattle of cow horn; the other beat a small drum. A line formed behind a chief who was wearing apron, beads, and headband, chiefs first, then men and boys, then women and girls, some carrying babies. The dance started slowly, not much more than a rhythmic shuffle with everyone looking serious. The man beat the drum somewhat faster. The rattler kept pace. The dance became lively. An old chief who had walked with a cane went back to his place on the benches. Two women, well over seventy, friskily raising their feet and their elbows, cavorting and laughing, seemed to infect the whole troop. The leading chief waved his arms and stepped high, the children and young people stepped higher; a few kept on looking glum and just shuffling.

The rattle and drum beat were hypnotic. More and more joined the dance. The circle widened till it went round the stoves instead of between them. Women passed their babies to grandmothers on the sidelines so they could dance with more verve. Round and round they went many times, to the throb of the drum and the rattle.

Then they stopped, laughing and mopping their brows, and sat again on the benches. Two men took the large basket around and handed each person a slice of unbuttered bread and a fat, spicy cookie. Then with a big ladle and dipper they filled the shiny tin honey pails that each woman had brought with the starchy soup from the kettle. Each family retrieved its own pail and dipped into it with a spoon or with bread. The woman beside me smiled and generously offered to let me dip in with her.

Outside on the road I met Willie John, a Seneca, a spry seventy-nine. "The churches are losing their customers," he told me. "They never git so many people out to meeting as come to the Longhouse." We walked to the little house where he lived with another old war vet, a big man with one eye who didn't say a word. They kept their place fairly tidy, cooked their own meals, and both wore their hats in the house.

"Couple times a year our chiefs preach our sermon," Willie said as he sat by the stove. "It takes four days to say the whole thing, beginning at six in the morning and stopping when the sun is halfway up the sky. Not wrote down and all learned off by heart in verses like the Bible. Young chiefs taught by old chiefs." Willie shook his head slowly. "Takes lots of learning. Iroquois scripture was give us by Handsome Lake, a chief of the Senecas. Round about 1800 he took out a hunting party one day and they went to the trading post and give skins for barrels of whisky, the first the braves ever had. They went back home in their canoes and got pretty wild, whooping and hollering and breaking down doors so their kids and wives got scared and ran away into the bush.

"When Handsome Lake noticed what a bad thing he done to his Indians he repented night and day for four year and at the end of that time four angels came and stood in the doorway with their feet off the ground and said they come from the Creator to take him on a trip.

"They took him along a wide road that went down to a building with no windows and so long they couldn't see the end of it and inside they could hear people yellin' something fierce like the devil was torturing them. The angels said, 'This is hell and the devil won't let no one out of it.'

"And then they took Handsome Lake to a different road, real narrow with the traces of children on it leading to heaven. It was just like here only brighter, no night at all, and the angels says, 'Listen to this,' and in a big building they were having religious sermons and dances, real lively. And the angels asked the chief was he thirsty and he said he believed he could drink and they give him a little dipper of water that kept filling up the more he drank out.

"And on the way home they told him how to make medicine and to be kind to the aged and never strike children, and if your husband strays take him back without anger, don't gossip or listen to gossip, and all the things that are in the Longhouse sermon. And the angels told Handsome Lake to go round and preach it to all the Indians. He preached for the rest of his life and that's what all the Iroquois Longhouses believes in," Willie John said. "It's not pagan, not idolatry like the white people say; it's pure Protestant religion, will take you to heaven when you die, if you live by it."

I spoke to many of the Iroquois about the Longhouse religion. In those who were Christian I sensed a consciousness of superior enlightenment but also a tinge of nostalgic envy of those of their race who had kept the faith of their fathers and remained truly Indian. They told me that the people of the Longhouse were the best-living people among them: sincere, kindly, sure; and schoolteachers said Longhouse children were the best-behaved pupils, respectful and honest. Josephine and Sylvanus General, a young Christian Mohawk couple, said they'd like their son, Joe, to go back to the Longhouse.

I spent a day with the Generals. Josephine called Sylvanus from the potato patch and we sat by the pump and chatted till too many caterpillers fell on us from the tree overhead and Josephine invited me to come into the house, "If you don't mind the baby chicks in the kitchen."

Sylvanus was a big man with plump cheeks and a slow, lazy smile; he farms and writes poetry. Josephine, tiny and bright, with a pony tail and slant-eyed spectacles, told me she was a city Indian, born in Buffalo, New York.

Their house is the oldest on the reserve and they love it. Made of red pine logs two feet square, it has one big room downstairs and one up, plus a lean-to. Josephine wants a new floor because it is cold in the winter; she talks too of adding French doors and a porch, but they haven't got round to it yet. They've been there eight years and can't make up their minds if they want to stay or build a new place where they wouldn't get so much dust from the road. But they can't get a mortgage or loan to help them finance it because the reserve is Crown land.

They don't feel secure: any day the government might take the reserve away from them – it often has tricked them before – so why go to a lot of trouble fixing a place up, only to lose it? They live one day at a time, they say, and don't worry about the next one, but they talk about it incessantly.

They constantly contradict themselves. One minute they say they live like kings, have privileges that the poor whites can't enjoy; next minute they are miserable slaves under Canada's Indian Act. They say no Indian can go out into the white man's world and cope with his cunning; then they boast that many of their people have left the reserve to become rich – doctors, lawyers, and one brigadier. Josephine was brought up a Roman Catholic, Sylvanus an Anglican; now they both think they'd like to belong to the Longhouse. But they've had too much education to believe in Longhouse witchcraft or medicine rites. So what should they do?

Josephine set the kitchen table for lunch. With the chicks peeping in their corner we ate canned corn and beans, bread and butter, sardines, store doughnuts, and cookies with pink marshmallow icing while they apologized for not giving me real Indian food like corn soup, which takes a day to prepare; corn bread, heavy but nourishing; delicious corn cakes and pudding, or sweet corn steamed in the husks.

We were still drinking tea at the table when Joe, a handsome boy of eight, came home after school with his friend Gordie Buck carrying a rattle of cow horn. Without any prompting Gordie sat on the edge of a chair and said, "Fish dance." Then he sang a weird, wordless Indian song and kept time with the rattle while Joe solemnly danced in a circle. "War dance," Gordie commanded and Joe's antics changed. Buffalo dance, Women's dance, False Face dance followed, the children performing the dances seriously and without any words. Sylvanus, watching, said dreamily he'd like to open a school to teach Iroquois dances and languages.

"But how can you, Sylvanus?" Josephine asked. "You can't dance and you only know English." She sipped her tea daintily. "I'd rather sell Indian handicrafts to get money to build a stone fireplace."

"But no one makes handicrafts any more," Sylvanus smiled his slow, lazy smile. It is hard to earn money on the reserve, he told me, for there is no kind of industry. It isn't in the Indian's nature to be greedy and competitive like the white man; he longs only for the wisdom of understanding and the betterment of his soul.

Old Ezekiel Hill got enough money from his bead work to buy a tiny log house for fifty dollars and have it moved up near the Seneca Longhouse. The plaster came out of the chinks in the moving and it let in the wind, but he stopped it up on the inside and it wasn't too bad in the winter if he kept himself covered with blankets. He wondered at first what he'd do for water and wood because he couldn't get out of his wheelchair except to roll himself to his bed, but a neighbour came every other day and looked after him so he had nothing to worry about outside of his rheumatism.

Ezekiel rummaged in the boxes on the table, which held the remains of his breakfast and supper, to show me the bead work he did with his crippled hands. There were belts with Union Jacks and American flags, headbands and necklaces with flowers or the words "Mother's Day" worked into them. "But nobody round here wants bead stuff no more," Ezekiel told me. "Only tourists sometimes comes in and buys 'em. Everything's changing from what it were. Indians is wearing underwear now, even the old folks. Days gone by people didn't work hard, they just lay around and they always had plenty. They made axe handles and baskets that they traded for food. Now just a few know how to make 'em. They used to go out and cut poles if they felt for it, then come in and sit or play games by the creek. Nowadays they get into cars and go into town to the pictures.

"Can't play snowsnake on the roads any more with cars running round." Ezekiel sighed. He leaned far over in his wheelchair to search in the piles of odd things on the floor. He pulled out a snowsnake, a slim, steel-tipped stick, highly polished, that is speeded along a track in the snow for perhaps half a mile if icing conditions are favourable and a man's arm strong and skilful.

"Nowadays kids can't play round like we used to, they got to go to school every day and get such learning put in their heads they got no room for Indian language." Ezekiel shook his white head. He never learned how to read or to write. He went to school when he felt like it – about one day a month.

Now all the Six Nations children go regularly by bus to one of the fifteen schools on the reserve; each school teaches one grade. The books, bus fares, and teachers' salaries are paid for by the federal government. One hundred fifty pupils are taken every day to the high schools in the nearest town, where they learn to mingle with white people and often surpass them in academic results. All the teachers on the reserve are Indians who hold first-class certificates and use the Ontario public-school curriculum, with an extra bit of Indian history.

"It isn't easy for us to teach our history from the school textbooks," I was told by Reg Hill, a soft-voiced Indian teacher who graduated from Upper Canada College. "The source material was written by our enemies, the French. When they attacked us they were at war; when we attacked them it was a massacre. They called us bloodthirsty savages, not braves fighting for our lives and our lands."

Reg Hill said the white man has never written the truth about the Iroquois. The French maligned them; the British have never given them their due. The Iroquois held the balance of power that won Canada from France; Canada would have been lost to the Americans in the War of 1812 if the Iroquois hadn't defended it.

"I'm always especially annoyed at having to teach that Brock, the British general, was the hero of Queenston Heights," the schoolteacher said. "He was a defeated leader. He led his men into an open field and ordered them to climb an unscalable cliff while the Americans fired at them from above. His soldiers fled and the battle was lost. It was the Iroquois, spearheading the Canadian militia of pioneers, who routed the Americans and saved Canada for itself."

Another teacher irked by textbook history was Miss Emily General, a sister of Sylvanus, whose dark hair was a yard long. She once travelled to Europe on a Six Nations passport and studied Iroquois records in England. She taught school for twenty years on the reserve but was asked to resign because she wouldn't take the oath of allegiance to Canada that all teachers were required to take in 1947. Now she raises turkeys and pigs and produces the Indian pageant each year in the Great Pine Forest Theatre at the back of her mother's farm.

The pageant re-enacts the life of an Iroquois hero or some phase of Iroquois history – this year Handsome Lake, the Seneca prophet revered by the Longhouse, and Pauline Johnson, the poet of the Six Nations Reserve. Everyone who has buckskins and feathers is asked to take part and they all do so freely and happily because it helps to keep real and alive the traditions of the Confederacy.

Emily General is fiercely jealous of the sovereignty of her nation. She believes, as do most of her people, that their Creator gave the Iroquois a big space to live in and it wasn't to be bartered or sold. The people of the present generation are only custodians of the lands of those not yet born.

But what heritage have they left to pass on to their children? the Iroquois ask as they look at their flat, meagre country with the dust rising thick on the roads. Will the greedy white man who covets all that he sees deprive them even of that? The Iroquois believe so. They live with their fears, their cars and TV sets, and their dreams of the green, wooded hills and the lakelands that their fathers had before them. But they'll keep on fighting for their rights. The Iroquois haven't been conquered.

On my way off the reserve I stopped to say good-bye to Chief Henhawk. He was sitting on his little back stoop with a notepad on his knee on which he was laboriously writing. He smiled when he saw me. "You're just in time to give me a hand with this here," he said.

"What is it?" I asked him.

"I'm writing a letter to the Queen. I'm asking her to give us back our freedom."

Maclean's, November 12, 1955

In May 1982, I drove to Ohsweken for the first time since I'd stayed there in 1955. The road into the reserve from the highway was paved, so was a crossroad; the gravel roads were wider and improved. In some ways the reservation was unrecognizable to me: as well as numerous painted clapboard and aluminum-sided houses there were many fine large homes with two-car garages and broad landscaped lawns; the tar-paper shacks that had once been common were gone, the few one-room log cabins were boarded up.

Ohsweken had grown. There were new public buildings: a government administrative centre, a community hall, an arena, a day-care centre, a drug and alcohol centre, a medical clinic. The old hospital had become a senior citizens' nursing home, the old council house, a library. There was still no bank, no high school, no liquor or beer store, no supermarket.

There were several new churches on the reservation. The four Longhouses, I was told, were as well attended as ever they were. Quite a number of the young people who belonged to the ancient Iroquois religion had teaching certificates and university degrees; many worked in the administrative centre, in the schools, and the social service buildings in Ohsweken. Mohawk and Cayuga conversation was taught in the schools.

"Do many people on the reserve still want to have an independent Iroquois country?" I asked everyone I spoke to. The answer was always the same: "I don't know, I suppose there are still some who do."

Sadly I learned that old Chief Bob Henhawk was dead; so were Reg Hill, Willie John, Ezekiel Hill. Alma Green, who had written several books of Indian lore and personal memories, was eighty-five and not well enough to do much but watch television.

I asked the way to the home of Sylvanus General. The Generals no longer live in the old log house they once loved. I found Josephine and Sylvanus in a large, very comfortably furnished, modern home on the 400-acre farm where they raise beef cattle. "Since the loans came through in 1959," Josephine said, "I don't see that we Indians have much to complain about." A system of borrowing and repaying money to build homes had been devised on the reservation and many people had benefited by it. Most of the fine homes I had seen, they told me, were owned by people working in the city of Brantford, or on high steel construction. "Not many are farming any more," Josephine told me, "except ourselves and our son Joe who has a chicken farm." Sister Emily is still raising pigs.

In November I spent a day with an Indian friend whose beautiful home on a bend of the Grand faces Chiefswood Park where for two days each summer Indians from all over Canada and the United States gather for a powwow to perform their native dances in traditional costume and to sell crafts.

The Unconquered Warriors of the Six Nations

My friend told me that the traditions of the Six
Nations are being nurtured in the schools of the
reservation and by teaching children and adults to
make Indian crafts in a large barn on her own farm.
In 1963 an arts council was formed on the reserve
and since then hundreds of children over the age of
nine have been taught to do leather and bead work.
Many of them, now grown up, have developed a
cottage industry which has enabled them to make a
living with the sale of deerskin jackets, moccasins,
gloves, purses, cornhusk dolls, silver jewellery with
clan symbols, corn soup, and corn bread. One young
woman maintains a supply store, and early in
November a bazaar is held in Ohsweken's
community hall.

Lacrosse sticks are still being made by one family;
there are still snowsnake competitions in the winter;
and in August every year, the Indian pageant is
presented in the woodland theatre on the reserve.

After lunch in the new Village Inn, my friend took
me to the Talking Earth Pottery, the restored log-
cabin studio where Steven and Leigh Smith make
traditional Iroquois pottery and exciting sculptured
pieces of their own creation, using symbols relating
to Iroquois philosophy and legends. Their work sells
so quickly that they seldom have much on display.

"Do you never make duplicate pieces?" I asked
them.

Leigh replied, "Oh no, that would be boring."

She showed me an album of photographs of works
they had created, shown, and sold in galleries in
Ontario and the United States. And on the wall of
the studio a framed picture of one of their
beautiful, unique pieces being presented to the
Queen.

Why the Amish Want No Part of Progress

*T*he Old Order Amish, I knew, had the same origins as the Mennonites: they travelled in buggies and had similar beliefs and lifestyles but considered themselves less worldly. In the winter of 1957 I stayed in their area to find out for *Maclean's* why these relatives of the Pennsylvania Dutch tended their farms without machinery, pulled out electric wiring and plumbing from houses they bought, had no churches, lived by rules laid down in 1525, and were happy living that way.

Men with bushy Old Testament-like beards and long Dutch-cut hair under broad-brimmed black hats are often seen on the main streets of Kitchener, Waterloo, and Stratford, Ontario. They wear "barn-door" britches (trousers buttoned across the top without zippers or flies); their suit coats, fastened by hooks and eyes, have no pockets, buttons, collars, or lapels. Their women wear coal-scuttle bonnets and long, plain dresses secured by invisible pins. Bundled in shawls, they ride imperturbably in topless buggies behind their plump horses while the world rushes by all around them.

These strange people are the peace-loving Old Order Amish (pronounced "Ah-mish"). By shunning conventional ways and trying to live as their ancestors did in 1525, they insulate themselves from the nuclear age to find everlasting security in their faith, their families, and their prosperous farms in Waterloo and Perth counties.

They spurn everything modern. If they buy farms with well-appointed houses they tear out electric wiring and bathroom fixtures, remove oil furnaces and telephones. They won't own a radio or a television set; musical instruments are taboo. They don't go to movies, will turn their backs on a camera, wouldn't ride in a plane. When asked why they won't buy a car, truck, or tractor, they reply, "Because the Lord didn't drive one when he lived on earth."

Not even the laws of the country can force the Old Amish to violate the teaching of Jacob Amman, the Swiss Mennonite preacher who founded the sect in 1693 by exhorting his followers to return to the ways of the Mennonite martyrs at the time of the Swiss Reformation. They won't go to court, won't swear an oath – and their word is accepted as their bond. They won't take up arms in a war – and Canadian law has exempted them from doing so. Though they pay taxes, they refuse old-age pensions and family allowances that might obligate them to the government and make them less independent. They won't vote in federal or provincial elections – they say they are too dumb. Their children stop going to school on the day they are fourteen because higher education might lead them away from the flock.

By being different and separate, the Old Amish claim to obey the biblical precept, "Be ye not conformed to this world."

Anything that is modern or fashionable they consider as worldly, therefore the work of the devil, and not for their use or enjoyment – but all right for anyone else. The Old Amish are humble, hard-working folk who quietly mind their own business and make no attempt to convert other people.

Unlike modern church organizations with their ever-expanding buildings, Ontario's ten congregations of Old Order Amish – about a thousand people – have no church buildings at all. For worship the Old Order gather in each other's houses or barns, and through services three hours long sit on backless benches that are taken from one meeting place to another in a horse-drawn wagon. They are sometimes called House or Barn Amish, to distinguish them from the more numerous and progressive Church Amish-Mennonites. Their preachers, chosen for life by lot from slips of paper drawn from a Bible, are farmers with no ministerial training but the reading of the Holy Book and of the stern Amish code based on the Bible's literal interpretation.

Obedience to their rules is severely imposed. If a baptized member of the sect fails to comply with its various regulations he or she is liable to be "placed in the ban." Such people are excommunicated from the church, not allowed to eat at the table with their families or sleep in beds with their spouses; fellow church members do not drink or eat with them or take anything from their hands until they repent of their sins, and are allowed back into the congregation by a vote of the members.

Rigid austerity is the rule of the Old Order Amish. Upholstered comfort and decoration are not allowed in their homes: floors have no carpeting, windows have no drapes or frilled curtains, walls have no pictures or paper.

The style of Old Amish clothing, prescribed by the traditions of their sect, has not changed in three hundred years. The men's coats are buttonless as a protest against the ornamented uniforms of mediaeval militia; that is also why the married men wear beards but no moustaches, and parting and clipping their hair is prohibited. Not to be tempted by fashion, the women wear plain clothes made from an identical pattern; cosmetics and all jewellery are forbidden. Their hair, never cut or curled, is centre-parted and drawn tightly into a knob,

137

always covered by a kerchief, an organdie cap tied under the chin, or a coal-scuttle bonnet, because women's heads should be covered when they pray and they might pray at any time and anywhere.

Though the Old Amish look pious and have many self-imposed deprivations, they seem to enjoy life. They love getting together to talk. Every Sunday they visit each other by the dozen; hundreds of them gather at auction sales, barn raisings, funerals, and wedding feasts. At their quiltings and at the Sunday-night singings for their teenagers they have hilarious fun: they play boisterous games and are practical jokers. With bags full of treats they love to go on a train to visit American relatives.

About fifty thousand Old Order Amish live in the United States. In Pennsylvania, where they first settled when they left Europe, they are the most colourful part of the Pennsylvania Dutch culture and are advertised as a tourist attraction. Many books and stories have been written about them; a musical comedy, *Plain and Fancy*, has been most successful; their images and folk art appear on greeting cards, pottery, and souvenirs. Amish delicacies – shoofly pie, seven sours, and dried-corn soup – are served in the restaurants of Lancaster county. But the Old Amish who live in Ontario are unexploited and almost unknown.

One day I drove twenty miles northwest from Kitchener to the heart of the Old Amish country where the fields are rich with manure, the houses are large but undistinguished, and the names on the mailboxes are frequent repetitions of Keupfer, Albrecht, Nafziger, Jantzi, Jutzi, and Zehr.

In the villages of Milverton and Millbank, where the Amish farmers shop and do business, I encountered an attitude of respect for and kindly amusement at Old Amish customs. I was told that, despite their strict rules, the Old Amish do some things that seem not unworldly. They make and drink cider and beer; some smoke cigarettes. Though they don't own cars, they will ride in them. They'll enjoy a non-Amish man's radio; they will "borrow" his phone. Some turn up regularly at a neighbour's house to watch television; they laugh loudly at the commercials, some like the fights, others prefer ballet and opera, and one red-bearded Amish man never misses a ball game.

"Inconsistent?" a Milverton businessman said to me. "They're only human. You couldn't find better neighbours."

"They never get into any trouble," a grey-haired by-stander told me. "Some of the young ones might like to kick over the traces but the old ones keep them in line."

"Sometimes I envy them," the businessman mused. "They seem to have real contentment."

To find out how they achieved it I spoke to an Old Amish bishop who had retired from farming but still performed his church duties of marrying, baptizing, banning, and burying. He was a short, square man with a smiling round face surrounded by black whiskers. He wore dark overalls and rubber boots that came up to his knees. He told me very kindly that the Old Order Amish do not like publicity and he was afraid his people would criticize him if he gave information about them. He said all their ways that seem strange to outsiders were direct biblical commands or could be traced to the days when their ancestors were persecuted in Europe. "And if you want to know about that you can read it in books," he said as he turned his broad back and strode firmly away from me.

I called on a young Amish couple who seemed delighted to have me come to stay with them to learn how they live, but when I went back three days later they said their parents had told them not to have me and I'd better go to some of the old ones who were wiser.

They directed me to the house of Sam and Leah Keupfer, an Old Amish couple who live in a *doddy* (grandfather) house, a few rooms attached to the large old farmhouse they once occupied but – in accordance with Old Amish custom – have now given over to their youngest son and his family. Leah, a wiry little woman wearing a black dress and apron with a black kerchief tied under her chin, invited me eagerly into her small kitchen-living-room, which seemed to be filled by her husband, Sam, as he stomped around in his barn boots, his patriarchal beard and long, grizzled hair streaming under a great, dusty black hat.

"Sit you, sit you," he welcomed me and gestured with his enormous, work-hardened hand towards several plain wooden chairs lined up against the green-painted walls. The room had no drapes, no pictures, no floor-covering but a piece of linoleum and a handmade rag mat. There was nothing unuseful but flowering plants in tin cans on the window sills and bits of cherished cheap china and glass tucked away in a large corner cupboard.

With his knees wide apart the old man sat on a hard black leatherette couch while his wife kept moving back and forth between a dry sink and an oilcloth-covered table. "You'll haf to excuse me if I keep working" – she smiled at me – "but one of ours is in the hospital and I'm making a meal to send over for her man and the kids. Our Joe is coming to fetch it."

"The word of God teaches us that we should all help each other." Sam was a retired preacher.

"That way we got nothing to worry us," Leah said. "If we get sick or old our children and relations will take care of us; if we get poor off they will feed us; if a widow loses her man our men will take in her crops and help with her chores." Leah smiled securely. "The good Lord looks after us good."

"What if something happens that wipes people out, like a fire or storm?" I asked.

"The word of God teaches us that when one member suffers all the rest suffer with him," Leah said.

"We have our property and stock valued and when there's a loss we all pay enough to cover it according to how much we've got," Sam explained. "It's just like insurance only, because we pay after the loss, we have no money on hand and are not a company and it is not a gamble. All the two or three thousand Church Amish in Ontario and ourselves are in it together, so no one has to pay very much and maybe only every few years."

At the shiny coal-burning cookstove Leah lifted the lid of a large iron kettle where smoked ham and dried apple segments (*schnitz*) were simmering; she gently dropped in some dumplings (*knepp*). "I'll keep enough out for our dinner and you can stay with us," she offered me, a stranger.

The sound of a tractor in the lane sent her to the window in a flurry of pleasant excitement. "Here's Joe already," she announced.

A man, bearded, long-haired, and in Old Amish clothes, came in and talked with his parents in the Pennsylvania Dutch dialect. When the dumplings were cooked Leah ladled the *schnitz und knepp* into a pot. Instead of handing it to her son she put the pot on the doorstep and he picked it up from there to take it away on his clattering machine.

Old Sam sensed the question in my mind. Embarrassed, he explained, "Our Joe married a woman that belongs to a congregation of Old Order that decided if God created man smart enough to make tractors He must have wanted them to be used." Sam looked stern. "We don't think it's right and we don't have much to do no more with that bunch of our people."

"Except our Joe," Leah added.

"We believe if people let all these new contraptions do their chores for them they won't have enough work to keep them busy and safe from trouble," Sam said.

"And we ain't bothered with salesmen; we just tell them what they got is against our rules," Leah told me.

Sam grinned. "A vacuum-cleaner peddler came here one day and Leah says to him, 'It's no use showing it to us,' but he got his machine together anyhow. And did we ever laugh when he looked around and said, 'Where do I plug it in?' He left pretty quick and there ain't none been around since."

Leah set the table with horn-handled knives, three-tined steel forks, and unmatched china. Sam dipped water from the stove's reservoir into a basin, washed his hands and face, took off his hat, combed his long hair and beard, then sat at the head of the table. We bowed our heads silently till he sighed and said heartily, "Reach for whatever you like," and helped himself first to the dumplings.

After dinner Leah took me through a door that led into the main house where her twenty-six-year-old son Noah lived with his wife, Catherine, and their children, Christian and Magdalena, aged three and four. The pregnant little wife, wearing glasses and the plain garb of the Old Order, welcomed me to her brown-varnished kitchen. The children giggled shyly and hid their heads behind her skirts till she said, smiling, "Ach, you sillies, go and play once." Then they leaned over the woodbox beside the stove and peeked at me under their arms. The pretty little girl's shapeless grey flannel dress was covered by a navy-blue apron; her hair was slicked into tight narrow braids tied together with string. The little boy wore a home-made collarless shirt and long Old Amish britches.

"We're awful fond of our mommies and don't like to get too far away from them." Catherine explained why the Old Amish live in settlements. "I guess we never get over it, even when we get old." She smiled fondly at Leah, who added, "Besides, we don't like to have to drive our horses too far for divine service and to visit each other or to help with the threshing and butchering, or if somebody's sick."

"And it's better for us to be all together like to keep our own ways," Catherine added.

"You live so close to town," I said. "Do none of your people ever leave home to get jobs there?"

Leah looked shocked. "They daren't. Not if they do what the Lord says. They got to be farmers. It says it right in the Scriptures that we should look after the earth."

"We wouldn't know how to do anything else," Catherine said, "and we wouldn't want to. We love making things grow."

Her husband, a slight man with bright eyes, came in and smiled at me shyly. "Noah has been ploughing," Catherine told me. "It takes him longer than those that got tractors but he loves to walk with his horses."

Noah sat on a wooden rocking chair, rolling a cigarette while both children ran to him and perched on his knees. Leah excused herself to go back to the *doddy* house to get on with her work. The children giggled and chattered. "Listen those kids jabbering in German," Catherine laughed. "They can talk English as good as we can. When we're alone we talk either the one or the other so they'll know both when they get to school."

"Ours ain't the High German," Noah explained to me. "It's the Pennsylvania Dutch like the Mennonites talk."

"Only it's just a little different yet," his wife said. "My grandfather told me his grandmother used to speak French."

"But they talked German too, because in the early days they got chased pretty well all over that part of Europe," Noah told me.

He explained that the Amish are an offshoot of the Mennonites, whose creed began when the establishment of a state church in Switzerland was opposed in 1525 by a group of scholars who wanted religious freedom. Members of the sect for many years suffered great persecution, torture, and exile; always resisting, never fighting, they fled from one place to another. They were still having trouble when, in 1693, Jacob Amman, a young Mennonite preacher living in Alsace, got the notion that the church was lacking in discipline and urged his followers to return to the ways of its earliest martyrs. He preached that the faithful should not be yoked in marriage or in organizations with unbelievers and revived the practice of *Meidung* (the ban). Amman's separation from the Mennonite church spread into north Switzerland and Germany and soon was carried to Pennsylvania.

"The first Amish man that came to Canada was from Bavaria," Noah told me in his low, drawling voice. "He landed in New Orleans in 1822 and walked most of the way to Waterloo County, where he picked out some wilderness that he thought would make a good place for a colony. Then he went to the governor of Upper Canada to ask him if it would be all right to bring people over here. The governor said, 'Go ahead,' but the Amish man was taking no chances – he went right to the palace of the king of England and got it in writing with a gold seal that the land would really be his."

Catherine smiled. "Then people came over and had families and spread out and that's how we're here."

The young couple and I chatted all afternoon. They asked me innumerable questions: how old I was, what I did in town, what I thought of taxes. The young woman showed me the man's *muhtze*, a tail coat, which was made of dark serge and would probably last him for church services, weddings, and funerals as long as he lived – "Unless he gets fat." She laughed. She showed me her black bonnet and the dainty white organdie prayer cap with its finely pleated back that the little girl wears for church.

They told me that the preaching is held every other week in the homes of church members. The men sit on one side of the room, the women on the other. A song leader starts off the unaccompanied hymns; there are two or three sermons by the preachers and bishop. There are no church dues; the deacon

collects the offerings and the money is put in the bank and distributed when it is needed among the poor of the congregation.

"But we don't have many that's poor off," Noah said, "or
rich either."

"We got one that has plenty." Catherine grinned impishly at
Noah.

He laughed and explained to me, "Our main aim is to raise
good crops and fine cattle and to save money to buy farms for
our children so they can get a good start when they marry, but
this man has only one daughter and she's an old maid."

"She's only a couple years older than we are," Catherine
told me, "and before we were married she tried to get Noah."

I called at the sprawling brick house of the Amish man who
owned fifty cows and all the land along one mile of road.
When I knocked at the door it was opened by a sullen-faced
older woman who reluctantly let me come in. She looked
disapprovingly at my grey kidskin coat and said, "I suppose
that is mink?" Her daughter, twenty-eight, wearing the little
prayer cap of the unmarried women, was sweeping the large
kitchen floor; the mother took the broom from her and thrust
it viciously under the stove.

"Ach, mama, I wish you wouldn't do that," the daughter
said. "You know if you work hard you'll be sick again."

The mother glowered as she swept round the chair I sat on.
"I can't sit around when there's work to be done."

Neither woman spoke to me voluntarily. The daughter put
two old-fashioned irons to heat on the stove; the mother
emptied a basin of water into a slop pail, then pulled on a pair
of rubber boots, folded a shawl over her head, and said, "I'll
hunt the eggs." She gave the young woman a look that said,
"You be careful."

While her mother was gone the daughter was more friendly.
She told me that though she hates going to the nearby cities of
Kitchener, Waterloo, and Stratford, she had once enjoyed a
trip by car to Indiana to visit some Old Amish there. She
showed me the embroidered patches of a "friendship quilt"
she was collecting, and a crocheted pineapple pin-cushion she
had made for her dower chest. She told me of the Sunday night
"singings" where the young people gather to get acquainted

and to learn the complicated hymn tunes of their people. But when I asked her about the pairing-off games they play, she snapped, "We don't tell about that," and busily ironed a flannelette petticoat without speaking to me for a while.

Then, "Would you like to look at our hymn book?" she asked me.

She brought me a copy of the *Ausbund*, the oldest Protestant church hymnal in use in America, compiled in 1564 and written by martyrs awaiting their deaths. It is printed in German without music, its tunes having passed orally from generation to generation, defying both rhythm and time. Some of its hymns have as many as seventy-four verses and take more than an hour to sing in the doleful one-part drone that sounds like the chanting of monks. Some of the hymns are long discourses on doctrine. Hymn 140, with thirty-two long stanzas, describes in detail the story of Hans Haslibach of Berne, his imprisonment and torture, and the prophecy that at his death three signs would prove his innocence: when his head would be severed from his body it would leap into his hat; the sun would turn red; and the town pump would flow crimson. Another hymn describes the trial and death of Michael Sattler, a former monk turned preacher, who because he had opposed infant baptism and warfare had his tongue cut out; his body, pinched and torn with red-hot tongs, was then burned at the stake.

The tenacious way in which the Old Order's refusal to conform has been maintained in compact agricultural-industrial areas probably comes from the strong sense of martyrdom that is seared into their memories, holding them together and making them look with apprehension and disapproval at the wicked ways of the world.

The daughter told me that the Old Amish used to make their own coffins but now they get them from the undertaker and sometimes they're a little too fancy. She said the casket is taken on a horse-drawn wagon to the graveyard and there it is buried by the relatives of the deceased. There are no monuments in the cemetery. The graves are marked with small slabs on which are engraved only the two initials of the dead. There are no family plots: "There's just rows and rows," the daughter said. "One for little children and babies, one for half-grown kids, one for single people, one for married ones that ain't old, and one for the old folks."

She folded a towel she had ironed and put it away in a drawer. As she worked she kept looking out the window towards the road, seemingly hopeful that someone might come up the long lonely lane.

Finding marriage partners among the Old Amish is not always easy. Their numbers are limited; first cousins may not marry; no converts are sought; and every year a few young people are excommunicated for choosing mates from the progressive Church Amish-Mennonites on neighbouring farms. But courtship is greatly encouraged, hopeful young visits are exchanged between the American and Ontario Old Orders, and the sect is increasing through the natural growth of large families.

I called back at the farm of the Keupfers several months after my first visit there. Though it was a cold day in January, Leah was outside on a ladder cleaning the windows of the *doddy* house. "Sam's in the barn," she called to me. "Go in to Catherine. I'll come when I finish."

In Catherine's kitchen a new baby lay sleeping in a spooled wooden cradle near the stove. "He played a trick on me." Catherine leaned over him fondly. "He came already before Noah could hitch up the horse and go for the doctor to drive me to town to the hospital."

Catherine welcomed me happily. "But you'll have to excuse me if my place ain't fit for company and if I keep working. I've got yet to trim wicks and wash all the lamp chimneys. We're getting ready for the preaching here on Sunday and everything's got to be cleaned."

"Then I shouldn't bother you," I said.

"You're no bother. It's not like getting ready for a wedding or a funeral; we don't feed them much – just bread and butter and jam and apple butter and cheese."

"How many will come?"

"Ach, now, I don't know right," Noah said from the rocking chair where he held little Magdalena on his knee. "We don't keep church records but I think we've got anyway eighty members in our congregation, don't you, Catherine? Then there's all the small children and those that aren't baptized yet. It makes quite a bunch; we set up the benches all through the downstairs of the house."

"Isn't it hard keeping all the little ones quiet during the long service?"

"Oh, no," Catherine said. "Those women that have small ones sit in the kitchen where they can get easy out back and sometimes in the second sermon we slip kids a cookie or a hard candy. But they have to learn to behave just like we do. That's good for them."

"Our children got to learn early to do what they're told," Noah said as he fondled the little girl who had fallen asleep in his arms. "As soon as they're old enough they each get their own chores to do round the barn and the henhouse. Magdalena's helping her mother already in the kitchen. When they're fourteen they quit public school and start working full time to learn how to farm and keep house. We believe the best way to keep out of trouble and happy is to keep always busy."

"Don't you sometimes envy the people who do all the things and have all the things that you're not allowed?"

The young couple looked at each other. Noah spoke. "We got the Lord's blessing and our home and our children and our farm nearly paid for, and we got all our friends and relations near us and nothing to worry about. What more could we want?"

Catherine said, "We're contented just like we are."

Maclean's, September 27, 1958

☆   ☆   ☆   ☆   ☆

Last summer I drove just beyond Milverton to call on the Sam Keupfer family, whom I hadn't seen since I'd written about them. The old house was covered with angel stone! There were two black cars in the yard, and a tractor sat near the large painted barn.

A young woman wearing a bright-green cotton dress and a prayer cap came out on the porch to greet me and invite me into the kitchen where I had formerly sat and chatted with her mother-in-law, Catherine.

She told me the old folks, Sam and Leah, had died a few years ago and now Catherine and Noah were living in the *doddy* house.

I sat on the couch and looked around: at the large refrigerator, a freezer, a big new avocado-coloured electric stove, various appliances, and a new baby.

"There have been some big changes since I was here."

The young woman grinned. "Oh, yes, we live more modern now, but the Lord is always the same."

"What about the Old Order?" I asked her.

"They don't change none. Some of us broke away but I guess there's more of them than ever, still living the same yet; they even got their own schools for the kids now." And she directed me to the home of an Old Amish farmer who has fourteen children.

Ile-aux-Coudres and the Inn of the Weeping Stone

I'd never heard of Ile-aux-Coudres until September 1958, when *Maclean's* sent me to write about the enchanting island in the St. Lawrence that keeps its ancient ways. I travelled there on a train that stopped at every sainted village along the river's north shore till it reached the Les Eboulements wharf where I got on a ferry that sailed two miles to my destination.

This piece was assigned by *Maclean's* but was not published. It was sold to *Canadian Home Journal* but that magazine was taken over by *Chatelaine* very soon after and the piece disappeared.

L ike a moat round a castle, the St. Lawrence River guards the odd and ancient ways of a stream-lined, lovely island that Jacques Cartier named Ile-aux-Coudres. Seventy miles below Quebec City where they call the river La Mer, it passively yields to the tides that bring to its elusive shore schooners, fish, seaweed, and guests for its summer hotel, l'Auberge de la Roche Pleureuse (The Inn of the Weeping Stone). Seven miles long and two miles wide, the island has two thousand people who speak archaic nautical French and live as their ancestors did by farming, weaving, and praying. The hotel has thirty-five rooms and two lively, youthful owners, Irma and Germaine Dufour.

A folder prepared by *les mademoiselles* to advertise their inn boasts of the island's charms in French and rather unusual English:

Far from noisey cities, in the quaintness of an enchanting scenery, visitors will greatly love the majestic nature. Right at the feet of the grand Laurentian Mountains is pure and invigorating atmosphere, long walks, salt water baths, fishing and hunting trips: ducks are plenty. And what's about good French Canadian cuisine, so well known to connoisseurs.

Jacques Cartier, who discovered Canada, has been likely the first white man on the soil of l'Ile-aux-Coudres. In September, 1535, he and his crew explored the island and due to the abundance of hazelnut trees, he called it l'Ile-aux-Coudres. When the holy mass was heard in the name of Christ and the king of France, he took possession of this portion of Canadian soil, cradle of our country. A memorial erected on the island, reminds us of this first mass celebrated in Canada.

Today in this still peaceful country, old stony houses remind to visitors, flowing each summer to the island, the old French Canadian living manners. Progress has left it unchanged; during his quietful vacation, in this sanctuary of the fatherland, he will constantly recall what was the French regime. And the very day he will leave l'Ile-aux-Coudres, he will surely wish to return. There he finds at once what his eyes, his heart and his mind are fond of.

A bus and the Canadian National Railways' daily service is operating from Quebec City to Les Eboulements wharf, where the island ferry sails many times every day.

Once in the morning and twice in the afternoon during the tourist season, the intrepid little six-car ferry crosses the channel from the mainland wharf to the quay built out from the tide-washed shore below the high plateau of the island. Two taxis swoop down to meet whoever comes on the ferry. A horse-drawn cart comes to pick up supplies. On both sides of the wharf are children fishing for smelts with long bamboo poles. *Goelettes* (schooners) loaded with pulpwood wait at the quay for the incoming tide to speed them upriver; their skippers sit in a row, chins in their palms. They spit out blobs of tobacco juice and mumble in French to the island's old-timers, who come to the quay for a yarn.

The white, diagonal gash on the wooded north side of Ile-aux-Coudres is a steep gravel road that climbs from the quay to the parish of St-Bernard-sur-Mer, whose painted wooden houses alternate with plum and apple orchards along a segment of the eighteen-mile road that runs round the rim of the island.

Turning right – west – to go the long way around the island, the road through the village passes stores in the lower front rooms of houses, gardens fertilized by seaweed, ox-carts, and outdoor ovens. It passes the Cartier Memorial Cross in a tiny flowering park, then a maple-sugar bush, that reaches to low land at the western end of the island – the parish of St-Louis-de-France.

On a slim, stony point that stretches towards Baie-St-Paul on the north mainland is a memorial to Père de La Brosse, the island's priest in 1765, at whose mysterious death the bell in the chapel at St. Louis was tolled by the hands of angels.

Through the scattered village the road runs close to a great stone church, a historic four-armed windmill, and two Norman pilgrimage chapels.

Going east along the south shore past reedy ponds and cedar swamp, the road runs close to the water, where fishing weirs form right angles in the sparkling tide and the gabled houses of the settlement of La Baleine peek over the edge of the high plateau above. It passes eleven wayside shrines where people may kneel and pray.

At the eastern tip of the island, l'Auberge de la Roche Pleureuse is aloof and alone. From the summit of Cap-aux-Pierres it looks down the broad St. Lawrence at Saguenay cruise ships and *goelettes* running up and down the river, at dignified liners and freighters on their way to and from the sea. Across the main channel, on the river's north shore, the village of St-Joseph-de-la-Rive clings to the edge of the land, and the houses of Les Eboulements climb a slope to the silver-spired church at the top of the nearest mountain. Beyond them a multi-coloured patchwork of field and forest spreads and fades to the rounded Laurentians. On the distant south shore of the river there is a range of misty blue hills dotted by little white houses.

The sprawling white clapboard inn with its broad veran-dahs, lovers' lanes, and lawn chairs was once a farmhouse owned by Cleophas Dufour, whose family have lived on the island for almost three hundred years. When his daughters grew up and realized that their home faced a scene of unusual beauty, they advertised it in the papers as a summer hotel.

"We start wit' not a penny, only two-three customer, and soon we have to build dis annex for thirty-five rooms," Mlle Irma said as she showed me around on the Saturday I arrived. "We couldn't pass over if we pay architeck so we plan it all ourself. My brodder make de dining room just like he make a bird-house, with ceiling look like a church. We stain de pine-wood and trim it with French blue, ain't it pretty?

"Everything we got is made on de island. De furniture in de lounge my brodder make with peeled cedar logs and de seats and back cushions we cover with *catalogne*, handwoven rag strips, like de drapes and wool rug on de floor. Dese big braided hats on de wall, Germaine and me make ourself: when Mr. St. Laurent, prime minister of Canada, stay here, he say dey're very nice. Everything we did ourself and we work hard."

Germaine, handsome and always laughing, stayed in the kitchen to cook; Irma, vigorous and bilingual, looked after the guests and the office.

All the guests for the holiday weekend came from Quebec City, Montreal, or somewhere along the river: a noisy party of twelve teachers, two tall, friendly young women, two prim, pretty ones who giggled and painted landscapes; a pleasant married couple, a blonde private secretary, a bachelor lawyer of distinction, a frisky little old Irishman who, like me, spoke a little French but couldn't understand it when it was spoken, a reserved English Canadian family, and a middle-aged widow who sighed, rolled her big brown eyes, and read a book called *Amour Humain*, which she clasped to her bosom whenever anyone came near her.

After a dinner of beef-steak and brown-sugar tart, a group gustily sang French folk songs round the piano; a few of us sat on the verandah to look at the moonlight on the river and to watch the *Empress of Scotland* sail by lit up like a palace giving a party.

"Look at dat moon," Irma called from the doorway. "Dat make de tide very high and good fishing. We got for you rubber boot if anyone want to go."

We walked to the nearest weir, a rectangular fence of brush woven smooth and close as a basket. As soon as the outrushing tide had almost exposed it, the farmer-fisherman and his son drove in a horse-drawn cart to the inner side of the angle; we followed on foot, splashing through tide-water puddles in the furrowed shale. In the moonlight and by the light of the fisherman's lantern we could see the trap, C-shaped and roofless, alive with flipping capelin, sardines, and smelts. The two men kept scooping them into the cart till it was more than half full; then they joggled back to the road where the fisherman's wife helped her men sort the fish and pack them into narrow wooden boxes. There were six hundred pounds of fish. "But dey don't make much money from dat," Irma informed us. "Dey mostly eat deirself or give to de neighbour. Fishing is only good for one week when de moon is big."

Early on Sunday morning everyone at the hotel was driven to mass, which was said in the twin-steepled grey stone church of St-Louis-de-France. The islanders came on foot, in cars, tractors, or horse-drawn carts, till all the benches and chairs in the aisles were filled and some people sat on the floor. The older women wore black hats and coats and were too devout to notice anything but the rosaries in their work-worn hands. The young ones, neatly dressed in home-made clothes, genuflected then solemnly followed the service.

Ruddy-faced, bright-eyed men in their shyly worn Sunday suits glanced covertly at the holiday strangers, who were trying to decipher the theme of the smoke-darkened murals near the ceiling. From the pulpit the aged priest in his long black robes urged parents to send their children to school – which began the next week – and to stay home with them in the evenings instead of visiting their neighbours, the island's only diversion.

When the church service was over people gathered in groups to chatter, and so strange was the islanders' ancient dialect that French Canadians from Montreal could hardly understand it. All the social life on the island, we were told, revolves around the church: there are no movies, clubs, or cafés; the highlights of life are provided by religious festivals. The main event of the winter is the Evening of Souls, when an auction-bazaar is held to raise money for masses for the dead. The middle of Lent is celebrated as Mi'Careme, a week of masquerading and fun in the manner of Mardi Gras. At Quarante Heures, the pious pray all night in the church, with a fifteen-minute interval every hour to smoke a pipe and gossip.

From the inn on Sunday afternoon we heard young islanders singing gaily as they trundled along the road in bough-decked carts. A group of young men who work on the mainland and were home for the holiday weekend came to the hotel's little bar. They drank till Irma thought they had had enough beer and jovially chased them away. When the tide came up the river, some of the hotel guests went swimming. The Irishman showed me la Roche Pleureuse, at the foot of the headland, on which the hotel was built; a flat-faced, dark rock with a spring in the ground above it and a declivity beneath into which water drips from the stone. The English Canadian family drove me with them to the boggy, wooded centre of the island to see an abandoned shed and tumbling racks that had long ago been used for drying peat to burn in fireplaces and outdoor ovens.

In the evening, Germaine and Irma invited the young islanders to come from the bar-room into the lounge; they cleared away chairs, tables, and rugs. The hotel's pretty maids dressed in Breton costume and took positions for *Les Plongers* (The Divers), a traditional island dance. Alphonse Bouchard, a handsome dark youth with a red kerchief knotted under his collar, called the graceful figures; merry little Paulo Dufour sat on a chair, played an accordion, and tapped the rhythm with his feet, till the tapping and the music and the screaming laughter of the whirling dancers infected everyone in the room. The widow, who sat by the blazing stump in the fireplace, kept twitching her slender ankles; the tall women, the lawyer, and the teachers joined the dance; the prim women watched and giggled; the Irishman danced a jig, and several young men of the island got up alone and clogged with the music and the fast, exciting, endless tapping of Paulo's fluttering feet.

When the holiday weekend was over all the guests left the hotel but the two tall women and the widow, whose sighs grew longer and louder as she finished her breakfast in front of the dining-room fireplace. A mist that was thick as a cloud had settled over the river and the constant blaring of fog horns told of anxious ships in the channel.

"Three time in last ten year big boats come on shore when fog is tick like dis," Irma said. "Dey throw deir cargo overboard and people here get free coal and barrel of flour." She poked the fire with a stick. "But today is nothing exciting, today no customer come to hotel." She shrugged her shoulders then said – very jolly and loud to defy the miserable weather – "Today I show you Ile-aux-Coudres. We walk, or ride on horse or ox or dog, anything dat will drive us."

As we crossed a stile in a fence that kept sheep, who wore wooden neckpieces, from invading the lawn of the inn, Irma said, "Everything on de island is very ol' fashion. People do everything for demself, build deir own house, build deir boat, mend deir shoes, make deir soap. Dey use to bake all deir own bread in outdoor oven but now a baker start business in St. Bernard and ovens are rusty."

We walked briskly to La Baleine, the little farming settlement whose houses straggled in single file along the southern plateau. "I want to tell dese people something," Irma said. "We will go in every house."

The first that loomed out of the fog had ten dirty, shy little children staring at us from the windows and the porch where a half-cleaned butter churn and a washtub of grey water made Irma turn up her nose. "But not in dis one." She rebelled.

"Dere are on de island only five woman dat are not clean, clean, and dey all come from over dere." She waved her arm towards the mainland.

We went into the next house, a square one covered with asbestos shingle. It had waxed linoleum on the floor, fresh, pretty paper on the walls, potted plants on the window sills, bouquets of cosmos on all the tables, and four little girls who watched us with solemn brown eyes.

"Dey feel bad because deir horse die las' night," Irma interpreted for me. "Dat's a terrible thing, you know, everybody need a horse to do de work, dey use more horse in Ile-aux-Coudres dan anywhere else in de country." Then she talked excitedly and angrily in French of the need for electricity on the island while the woman of the house kept quietly shaking her head.

"Dese people are crazee," Irma said when we were walking again. "Dey know nossing. Dey say dey don't want electricity because dey don't want de poles on deir land." Her voice rose and was louder. "But dey got poles all round de island for de telephone. See?" She pointed to one. "Most farmer have de phone and dey don't need. Dey have it just because dey like to listen in when deir neighbour speak together."

Loudly calling a greeting, Irma walked into the kitchen of every house without knocking. In almost all there were babies and the smell of cooking soup. On the walls were religious pictures, crosses, and images; painted horseshoes hung from raftered ceilings. At one place we saw a woman spinning wool from her own flock of sheep; at another, skeins of hand-spun linen thread hung on a fence to bleach. "Dey grow de flax and weave deir own towel and tablecloth like we got some at de hotel," Irma told me. "Dey never wear out for years."

We passed wayside crosses and religious statues with flowers growing around them. Several houses had sticks wound with cotton batting hanging on the screen doors, "To frighten flies away," Irma explained. "Lots of old-time hokus-pokus round here, but it don't work."

At every house we were greeted with welcoming smiles; at every house Irma preached the need of electricity. "I think maybe all on de island will want it but maybe five," she told

158

me. "Dose won't sign de paper because dey want to be de boss." She shook her fist in the air. "Dose are very dangerous men, dey say one thing on de front and anodder thing on de back. We must handle dem with de white gloves." She rubbed her thumb and fingers together. "One man I know is not good to his wife; when his horse have a baby he runs quick for de hot water, but when his wife have sixteen kids he runs for nossing." Irma so violently shook her head that one of the studded combs fell out of her smooth black hair. "I want no husband like dat," she said, "I like better to be independen' and go to Florida in de winter."

Near the end of the row of houses were two little, low Norman cottages of stone masonry three feet thick, built three hundred years ago by early settlers. "But ain't dat a shame?" Irma shouted when we stepped through the doorway of one. "People could still live in dis but dey let the chickens have." On the floor was a litter of rubbish and straw. The narrow board walls were painted cream and in fair condition; on shelves built near a deeply recessed window we found an old French Bible, a book about a Canadian exposition held in 1855, and a hen's egg. "And look at dis here," Irma exclaimed, holding up a queer little chair whose hand-carved back and legs were firmly set into a seat that had been a vertebral bone of a whale. "I must have dis for my hotel, it's a very old thing, very precious, from *la baleine* [the whale].

"My grandfadder tol' me seventy-four year ago de tide bring dis whale to de shore of the island. Everyone get excite because dey don't see such a ting dis far away from de sea; eight men go out in boat and kill it wit dose kind of old-fashion gun dat shoot stone. Dey get I don't know how many barrel of hoil from dat big fish but very much, and every family keep one of dese bone for souvenir and dey call dis shore La Baleine."

Gaily holding the chair on her head, Irma ran to the nearest farmhouse. She came out ten minutes later. "For many year I want to buy dis but dey won't sell; today I got for five dollar. Dey say I can leave and call for it tomorrow but I take no chance, tomorrow dey might change deir mind. People on de island is funny dat way, if anybody come here from de States and offer dem fifty cents for dis or anything, dey take it but if I want it to show my customer de old tings of de island, dey won't sell. But dis time I got." She swung her treasure round to carry it on her shoulder.

We ran down a plunging lane to the road along the shore; the mist had become a drizzle and we jogged back to the hotel.

The next morning was sunny, and Irma announced that we would go to St. Louis, at the other end of the island.

"Are we taking the horse?" I asked her.

"Too far for de-horse," she said, "we walk."

As we trotted along Irma kept saying we might be picked up by a car, but none came. We'd walked several miles when a man on a tractor gave us a lift.

We called at the first house in St. Louis, a new little cobble-stone cottage whose blue-eyed young mistress gave us sand-wiches and tea. "She is my cousin," Irma informed me. "Many peoples here is my cousin; on de whole island dere is only six-teen different names. All de families was here for over two hundred year. Except the doctor, he came last year; before dat de island have no doctor – but everybody is healthy."

On the little quay of St. Louis women and children were fishing and Paulo Dufour, the accordion player, was heaving sacks of cement from a wagon to the deck of a hundred-ton vessel. "Dey make many wooden ship like dat on de island," Irma said. "How dey make is a secret from way back in de family, and dey never tell dat to nobody. First dey make a small model" – she used her hands to illustrate – "den dey make it big like dat. When ship is finish dey have great celebration. De tide comes early in de morning, and all de peoples is here from de island. De *monseigneur* come from de mainland all dressed in fancy red robe; he sprinkle holy water and pray to bless de boat. De wife of de owner carry bouquet of flower and baptize with bottle of champagne. Den dey trow de boat on de water."

Almost everything in St. Louis can be seen from the quay or the road: houses, gardens, barns, a frame school painted brown. On either side of the great stone church are two white-washed ancient chapels with rounded backs and diminutive spires over their doors. Beyond a field of potatoes and a field of flax is the round stone windmill with a conical roof and four great wooden arms, now plugged into immobility. It was built by the monks in the late 1600s with walls four feet thick so it could be used as a fortress; its massive machinery, still in working order, ground the grain of the island until two years ago.

Monks of the Sulpician order were the first people to live on Ile-aux-Coudres. They came in 1689 and soon were followed by settlers who lived through turbulent times. Twice during the siege of New France, when the English came up the St. Lawrence, the terrified islanders fled to the mainland and hid themselves in the woods. In 1759 they were kept from their homes for two months while part of the English navy occupied their island. Then Nicette Dufour and Francois Savard secretly crossed the river, hid in a thicket near St. Louis, captured the grandson of the admiral of the fleet, and bargained for his return – and theirs.

Twenty years later there was another invasion. This time the marauders were worms, unbelievably large and horrible. Their number increased day by day till they covered all of the island. There were worms in the barns, worms in the wells, in the houses, the beds, in the soup; they ate the leaves off the trees, ate up the pasturage, the grain, and the vegetables. They covered the bodies of the animals and crawled on the children. Everyone turned supplicating eyes to the sky. The priest of the parish sent a delegation to the archbishop of Quebec to beg for a day of fasting. A mass was celebrated, a procession took place, and the very next day every worm on the island was dead. Moreover, a flooding rain fell for several hours and washed all the decaying creatures into the river!

Irma and I got a ride in a beer truck to St. Bernard parish, where everyone was out picking plums, little pointed blue ones and round yellow honey plums. The harvest was bountiful, everyone was merry; we were urged to fill our pockets, and we did.

Some of the farmers on the island have as many as two thousand fruit trees, from which they export thousands of baskets. "All dem are very good off," Irma told me. "Dey sell many potatoes and some strawberry too. Nobody is poor; every house have orchard, vegetable garden, and flowers. Dey all got a boat, a horse, cow, sheep, and some got a tractor, maybe fifteen on the island got a car or a taxi. In summer young men get job on *goelettes*, in winter some take job in Quebec or Montreal. Others come home to rest and dance, make love wit' de girl. De girl go not away from de island, dey make deir living at home."

We went into a shining mauve-and-yellow kitchen where a woman at an oil-cloth-covered table was cutting out something pink and lacy from a paper pattern. She led us to a corner stairway built into a space four feet square; we climbed the narrow, triangular steps to a bedroom where the woman's three daughters were making *catalogne* carpeting. One girl, perhaps fourteen, with curled blonde hair and dark-lashed blue eyes, very pretty, sat on the floor sorting and untangling long strips of rag; another, dark, with much lipstick, wound the rag strips onto bobbins that fitted into boat-like wooden shuttles; the third girl, older, thin and pinch-faced, was weaving: thrusting the shuttles back and forth at a hand-loom threaded with cotton warp.

"In many homes on the island they make *catalogne* like this," Irma told me. "It is very old-fashion French Canadian way to waste nothing; they cut or tear old clothes in strips to weave for carpets, drapes, or bedspreads, in different thickness and width."

The woman spoke rapidly in French which Irma explained to me. They get some rags from Montreal to make mats to sell in shops. For their work the girls get forty cents a yard; if they work very hard, three girls can make twenty yards of *catalogne* in a day. "But dey can't work dat hard very often," Irma told me. "Dey are too *fatiguée*."

That night when I asked Dezeange, the gentle little waitress at the hotel, what she will do when the hotel closes in October, she smiled and said, *"Rien."* Irma, who was typing in her office, said, "That girl is smart, she want to learn everything, she want to practise on dis typing machine, she want to play 'Frère Jacques' on piano, she want to go to city to hearn money and go more to school, but her modder and fadder keep her home to raise up deir odder seven children." Dezeange, who understands no English, walked out of the room and Irma went on, "One day she will marry and have seven children." So Ile-aux-Coudres goes on.

When the ferry was taking me back to the mainland, a cold wind blew up the St. Lawrence. Ile-aux-Coudres faded softly away and I thought of what Irma had told me when she asked me to come again. "In summer is dis island most beautiful in de world, but in winter is no place more lonely; de tide bring blocks of ice, de ferry stop running and nobody come or go, only de mans dat cross for de mail. Dey have big canoe wit' steel runner on bottom dat dey slide over ice, den dey slip in de water where dey make it go with de hoars, very, very dangerous, den dey pull up on ice again, den in de water till dey have cross two miles to Les Eboulements. Sometimes dey don't get dere; every year somebody is drown while deir wife wonder when dey come home. Dey wait here always very much for de springtime when tide bring again de *goelettes* and de fish – and we wait very much too for visitor to come to l'Auberge de la Roche Pleureuse."

September, 1958

Late in September 1981, when the Laurentians were scarlet and gold, I drove along the north shore of the St. Lawrence to St-Joseph-de-la Rive, where a ferry now waits every hour to take as many as sixty-five cars and passengers to Ile-aux-Coudres. I went directly to l'Auberge de la Roche Pleureuse, which had been expanded to accommodate two hundred fifty guests instead of the thirty-six it could care for on my first visit.

"Irma and Germaine are gone!" I was told by Eliane, the bilingual hostess. "Irma died two years ago and Germaine before that. They leave the hotel to their niece. But you see Irma and Germaine wherever you look."

The braided hats were still on the walls of the lounge; hanging beside the fireplace was the whale-bone chair; and there were framed photographs of the two sisters welcoming M. Pierre Trudeau, M. et

Mme St. Laurent, and other distinguished guests. "Before he was prime minister, Pierre used to come here for a week every summer; he still comes but too busy to stay so long."

I found the island as enchanting as ever: there are many new homes, five summer hotels, and chalets, electricity, and a flourishing peat-moss industry; though the *goelettes* no longer go up and down the river, they are picturesquely abandoned on the shore. Fascinating are the many *artisanat* shops selling *catalogne* and linens woven by the women of the island. "Everybody now has a loom," Eliane told me.

"What else do they do?"

"In summer is many tourists; all winter is nothing, just weaving, church, and bingo."

"And what of the little waitress, Dezeange? Did she leave the island?"

"No, she stay here. She is marry and have five kids."

The Village That Lives One Day at a Time

*I*n 1960 Doris Anderson, then editor of *Chatelaine* magazine, asked me if I'd write a series about the lifestyles of various families in Canada.

"Where will you start?" Doris wondered.

Well, naturally, Neil's Harbour. As always I wanted to go there; I wanted to tell about the family of Maggie's sister Jean: warm, vigorous, self-reliant, fun-loving, wonderful people who live on fishing and hope.

J ean and Owen Williams, with their five children, live in
Neil's Harbour, a sea-battered fishing village of three hundred people on the rocky north coast of Cape Breton, where
the average net income of a fisherman is a thousand dollars a
year. Though Owen's occupation is hazardous, Jean's work
never-ending, they love their life by the water. Jean says, "If
you're happy it don't seem to matter that you don't have
much money."

Jean has a pretty little five-foot-two figure, a piquant face,
and eyes that are always smiling as if she had a wonderful
secret. "Me and Owen's been married sixteen years and he's
just as much fer tarmentin' me now as he was at the start,"
she says shyly. "And he never gets mad at me. I only ever seen
him really mad once in his life – when he beat up on a fellow
that was bothering me."

Owen is a tall, quiet man with fine Celtic features and
brown eyes that are warm and good-humoured. He owns a
twenty-six-foot boat powered by a Chevrolet engine, and
whenever the tides and the storms don't prevent him he fishes
for lobster, mackerel, and codfish while Jean keeps running to
the window to see if his boat's coming in. "They don't go out
very far," she says, "but when it's thick-a-fog or snowing and
blowing they can't see the shore and I can't see them and it's
awful."

As soon as Owen comes safely back to the house in his rubber boots and long-visored cap she asks, "Did you get any?"
and almost invariably he shakes his head grimly and says,
"Not enough." It costs a boat owner like Owen eight dollars a
day for bait and gas; he gets only four cents a pound for his
fish, the price offered by the co-operative and the transient
buyers who truck the fresh fish away because Neil's Harbour
has no freezing or processing facilities.

Inshore fishing is becoming as obsolete along the Cape
Breton coast as are corner grocery stores in the cities. The
small boats that must be hauled up on shore every night and
launched with backbreaking effort every morning can't com-
pete with the large, company-owned vessels that can go out
where the fish are and stay for months at a time with their
catch in cold storage aboard.

Neil's Harbour once had fertile fishing grounds but for the

168

past three years the fishermen have caught very little. "It's the big draggers that's doin' it," Owen claims. "They come in three miles off our shore from Denmark, Russia, and Iceland, England, Portugal, France. They scrape the bottom and haul up everything that comes in their path, killing all the small fish and scaring the big ones that used to come our way. We can't make a living no more, no matter how hard we try. If I could get any other job I wouldn't go fishing, but with the national park hemming us in on the one side and the sea on the other, there's nothing to get around here. We can live cheaper in Neil's Harbour than anywhere; we got our own home, we can't move away from it – and we sure wouldn't want to."

The Williams's little white-shingle house has no plumbing, no upholstered furniture, rugs, or clothes closets; they have no car, refrigerator, or phone, but they don't miss what they never have had. They are thrilled with each new addition Owen has made to the home they're so fond of. It used to have only one room downstairs with two tiny bedrooms above it; now there's a kitchen and living room with three rooms upstairs. They have electric lights, an electric iron, and a washing machine that Owen has repaired many times; a hand pump brings water into the kitchen, an oil stove and a coal-burning cookstove keep the house warm; they have Jean's mother's old foot-pedal sewing machine and a brand-new TV set that they're buying on time and enjoying from noon until midnight. "We don't know how we'll keep up the payments," Jean says wistfully. "But we had to get it to keep the kids home."

Almost every night after supper Jean and Owen sit on straight-backed wooden chairs near the oilstove in their living room, Owen's arm around Jean's shoulders, her legs across his knees, like lovers at a movie, while their children, Freddie, fourteen, and Wilbert, ten, lie on the floor at their feet, and Donna, six, Norman, four, and Yvonne, three, perch in pyjamas on the stairway behind them. "I'd be some proud to get you kids upstairs," Jean says, and chases the little ones to tuck them into their beds for the second or third time.

Their television is, for the Williams family, a fascinating mirror of a world they've not ventured into. The city of Sydney is beyond Smoky Mountain and more than a hundred miles south; they don't have a chance to go that far very often. Neil's Harbour is so remote, isolated, and lonely that it is seldom visited by anyone but the relatives of people who live there. In the summer a quarter million tourists pass by on their way round the Cabot Trail, Cape Breton's scenic highway, but only one carload in two hundred drives into the village to have a quick look and take pictures.

Neil's Harbour is bleak but it's beautiful. Artists often paint the granite cliffs and the rocky point with the red-capped white lighthouse against the blue sea; they revel in the lobster traps, bobbers, killicks, and herring nets between the silvered-shingle storage huts (called stages) clustered round the shore, and the painted houses of the fishermen, with gables pointing to the sea where the fishing boats come in.

Every house in the village is like a watchtower perched on the slope of a high, treeless hill. From all the front windows can be seen everything that goes on along the roads, on the wharves, and on the sea to the far horizon. The back and side windows give intimate glimpses of small barns, outhouses, and the little paths that have been beaten through the rocky, weedy fields from one house to another. There is little privacy in the Harbour; everyone knows everything that goes on there. There are few phones, no telegraph system; news is carried more quickly over the network of paths, even when they are muddy or thigh-deep in snow drifts.

Neil's Harbour is just like a family: every one of the three hundred people who live there is a cousin or uncle or aunt of somebody else in the village – except the merchant (who owns the grocery store), the doctor, and the Anglican preacher. There are fifty Frickers; two-thirds of the rest are Seymours, Williamses, Buffets, Ingrahams, and Budges. Owen's mother had ten children, Jean's mother had thirteen; within sight of Jean's and Owen's house are the homes of both their parents and those of most of the brothers and sisters who have not left the Harbour.

Jean never has a chance to be lonely; every day from morning till night anyone who lives in Neil's Harbour might open her door and walk in without knocking. Sometimes there are fifteen people in the kitchen while Jean is doing the dishes or baking a pie, or washing her hair.

Little Freddie Warren comes with a note from his mother.

"Could you please lend me a pound of margarine until Friday," Jean reads aloud. "That's when Fred gets home from fishing. She won't have no money till then."

Jean's mother, Clara May Ingraham, comes in. "Where's that fellow in truck with the bootleg coal that Owen got some from? I got to get a ton; if I don't look after it nobody doos. If we runs out there's no way of gettin' it, we'd just freeze to death."

Jean's sister-in-law Sade sticks her head round the door and says, "Johnnie's just took Beat to the hospital on the hand sleigh to have her baby – the snowplough couldn't get up the hill."

Clara May says, "I better go right up there and make her dinner."

"I wonder if she got her wash out today," Jean says. "I could do it tomorrow and still get my cleaning done."

Jean has a regular routine for her housework. On Mondays and Thursdays Owen rolls the washing machine in front of the sink and fills it from the boiler on top of the stove, and Jean joins the race of all the women in the Harbour to be the first to have snowy sheets billowing on the line in the sea wind.

The kitchen floor is swept several times every day. "They brings in so much dirt on their boots," Jean explains, "and the kids always got such a stir-up." On Tuesdays and Saturdays she cleans the whole house. In the airy, bright bedrooms she wipes the dust from the three iron beds, the packing-case chests and the plastic curtains that hang in the doorways where there are no doors. In the living-room she washes the four varnished chairs and the child's table with a tall plant growing on it in a graniteware pot; she shakes out the blanket on the iron camp cot, dusts the TV set, the oilstove, and the shiny pink walls that have no pictures but a calendar, a pencil sketch of a boat that Freddie has made, and a small, fancy plate, made in Japan, with the Last Supper painted on it. She scrubs and puts wax on the linoleum-covered floors upstairs and down, then says to Owen or Freddie, "Run over to Matt's or to Mom's, dear, and borrow the polisher." And when she's all done she flops on a chair and says to her step-brother Fred, or to Owen, or to whomever is there, "Give me a cigarette," and they pass her the makings.

Jean has always worked hard. She had to stop going to

school when she was twelve because her family hadn't enough money to buy books to let her go on to grade ten. She cried and cried about that, then hired out to work at the minister's house for fourteen dollars a month. When she was fifteen she left home to work at Big Bras d'Or for a woman who drove the mail around Boulardarie Island in Bras d'Or Lake while Jean got up at five in the morning, made the kindlings, washed the clothes, set the bread, cooked, baked, ironed, and looked after three children and a baby. When she was nineteen she married Owen. She thinks of her wedding and the births of her five children as the glorious events of her life. And she joyously works harder than ever.

Friday is baking day in Neil's Harbour. Jean bakes muffins, cake, three pies, gingerbread, butterscotch squares, and a mountain of molasses cookies. "Seems like I can't fill 'em up," she says fondly. "They're always going after something." Three times a week she bakes nine loaves of bread, tea biscuits, cake and more cookies. "I just make them out of my head," she says. "You can't take time to be looking up recipes when you got a man and five hungry kids waiting for a meal at twelve and at five o'clock sharp."

For dinner Jean gives them potatoes and turnips or carrots with corned, dried, or fresh codfish, baked haddock with dressing, fish chowder, or boiled salt mackerel. They have baked beans every Saturday night and for breakfast next morning. For Sunday dinner there's roast beef with Yorkshire pudding; sometimes there is ham, fried bologna, corned beef and cabbage, or hamburg if they can afford it, rabbit pie, or venison in the fall if they're lucky. They seldom have lobster because Owen can sell what he catches for thirty-five cents a pound. Cods' heads, cheeks, tongues, and roe can't be sold and they are delicious when Jean stews or fries them. "Ain't it a good thing there's different fish?" Jean smiles. "We don't get much variety otherwise."

Neil's Harbour has only one store, the Lucky Dollar Foodmarket, which has a fair stock of staples, canned goods, and mixes, but Jean can't buy drugs, magazines, hardware, house furnishings, or anything else in the Harbour except cheap children's clothing and a few oddments from a truck that comes round to the houses. Most of Jean's shopping is done through the mail-order catalogues and comes parcel post; whatever is too big to come in the mailbags is sent up twice a week, except in winter, on the *Aspy*, a mine sweeper converted to carry freight to Cape Breton's north shore.

Jean resigns herself to making most of the children's clothing from cast-offs that someone has given her. She is glad that Owen's fashionable sister in Toronto wears the same size that she does and sends her clothes she no longer needs. When Jean dresses in the evenings or for church she wears a green woollen sack dress or a belted red jersey chemise; for square dancing she has a smart black sheath and earrings and necklace that make her feel as glamorous as the women she sees on TV.

Jean's social activities are limited. She teaches Sunday school and goes to the Anglican church every Sunday. She is a member of the Women's Auxiliary of the Neil's Harbour branch of the Canadian Legion and loves nothing better than the dances that are held in the hall by the members who swing with laughter and verve in the figures of the squares or merrily step-dance to the music of a fiddle, guitar, and accordion.

Saturday is hockey night in Neil's Harbour: no one misses the NHL games on TV. Jean and Owen and his brother, Stewart, and Bill Strickland sit on the straight chairs lined up below the stairway at the back of the living room; Fred and his wife, Inez, sit on the iron camp cot, and Freddie and Wilbert lie on the floor, aiming their toy guns at the players who oppose the Toronto Maple Leafs.

Every Wednesday night at seven-thirty Jean goes to her bingo, a club of ten women who meet in each other's homes and play for a fifty-cent prize. There is no bank in the village so the women bring their household savings to be kept by the club treasurer till they need the money for Christmas. "And some has saved up to sixty dollars in a year," Jean says admiringly. When she has the bingo at her house they play in the kitchen. She calls out the numbers then gives her guests tea, corned-beef sandwiches, muffins, and cake while they talk of what has been going on in the Harbour.

Jean's mother-in-law says, "Oh, my, when Owen's boat was

four hours late coming in in that glitter storm Stewart was that anxious and Hubert was all of atremble and they went out on the point to look for them."

"Whenever you see men out on the point by the lighthouse you know that it's bad," Beat Buffet says.

Jean tells them, "I could hardly hold myself still, I got on my coat and run over to Mom's and when they come in Owen said, 'What was you worried fer, it wasn't that bad out there.'"

"You never know what could happen to a man on the water," says Jean's sister-in-law. "Remember the day Peter Buffet were out in a dory and a man-eating shark tried to get him? Hit chewed at the rails and made marks on the rudder as if a saw had been at it. If he hadn't had a outboard on back and got away quick no one would have knowed what happened. A man in Louisburg got et by one last year."

Jean says, "And remember that time when Owen went out after seals on the drift ice and him and Jack Fricker got into a lake of water and it closed in around them and they couldn't move? They didn't freeze because they were trying so hard to work their way out of it, but it wasn't till eleven at night the ice shifted and they got in at White Point. I had no idea where they'd got to and nearly was crazy till I heard on the radio from Sydney that they was safe." She smiled. "And the next day he went out again and the ice blocked him in at Black Brook."

Winter can be cruel in Neil's Harbour. Three thousand miles of ocean crash against its cliffs and send spray flying over the road. The point is sometimes made an island by waves. The grey-shingle stages near the shore have often been moved by the storms. Boats have been smashed to kindling. The wharves where the fishermen land have been destroyed and rebuilt many times. The ten-ton concrete blocks of the breakwater have been tossed onto the government wharf by storms. Fifty-mile-an-hour gales shake the wooden houses and blow off their shingles. Jean always hurries along the sea road, she's so cold in her cloth coat and head scarf. "Coats seem to get thinner and thinner the longer you got them," she says, "but when you pay twenty dollars for one from the catalogue you got to wear it for six or eight years."

Spring comes reluctantly to the Harbour: its few lilacs

bloom in July. The earth is too shallow for gardens. The women clean their homes till they sparkle; the men paint their boats; and in May every man with a boat or a dory goes out on the sea after lobsters.

Summer is playtime in Neil's Harbour: it is drenched by the sun; the sea is calm and blue; the men fish for cod with hand lines. Relatives come home for their holidays, and though the housewives work harder than ever, there is much more fun. Jean's sisters and their husbands and children come home from Halifax, Sydney Mines, and Toronto. They have cars and take Jean and her family on picnics and out to pick berries. When her bachelor brother Ewart comes back in his new Pontiac, Jean goes with him to a dance every night in nearby Ingonish, Dingwall, or Cape North, while Owen stays home with the children.

"Hope they got a good lot of fish today," is the prayer of all the women in Neil's Harbour whose men go out on the sea in the fall; it is their last chance to earn money till May. "I don't know how we'll manage this year," Jean says. "Owen's trawl was washed away in the tides and it costs a hundred and fifty dollars to get lines and hooks to remake it. Yvonne got an abscess in her thigh that had to be cut and now we owe the doctor a good lot of money." Jean hugs Yvonne to her breast. "We could have lost her.

"I remember when Owen could make as much as five hundred dollars fall fishin'; we'd buy a case of margarine, a case of milk, a puncheon of molasses, and a lot of other things, and still have money left over for Christmas. But the last three years are so different, there's just nothing out there." Jean inclines her head towards the sea. "Owen hates to get relief or to borrow; he takes chances on fishing as long as he can in the blizzards. But most of December he just can't go out any more and we got nothing to live on but the baby bonus till Owen applies for unemployment insurance in January, when he'll get only twenty-one dollars a week."

Owen is never idle: at five every morning he kindles the fire, makes breakfast, and is out in his boat before the sun rises. When he can't fish he goes into the bush to cut firewood and saplings to make lobster traps, or he works on his gear. Sometimes he baits trawls till near midnight.

Like most men in Neil's Harbour he can repair his boat, fix its motor, make trawls and herring nets; he makes his own lobster traps, knitting the headings and making the hoops in the kitchen during the long winter evenings. He made his own snowshoes, handsomely strung with oxhide; with Kootch Fricker's help he enlarged his house and built modern cupboards. He can give a professional-looking haircut and cook a good dinner; he does innumerable chores round the house. But no matter how hard he works he always has time to let his little children climb up on his knees to hug him and kiss him.

"Ain't it awful to think of them getting big and going off and leaving us?" Jean says and the smile in her eyes is replaced for a moment by the lost look of anxiety.

"But we don't want the boys to go fishin'," Owen reminds her.

"What will they do? There's nothing else for them here."

All the little boys in Neil's Harbour want to be professional hockey players when they grow up. Wilbert practises constantly with his stick in the kitchen, on the road, and on the pond when it's frozen over.

Freddie plays hockey too. He has impish brown eyes and gold, curly hair and he loves to square-dance, to draw pictures of boats, to read books when the Cape Breton bookmobile calls once a month; in winter he sets snares to catch rabbits and in summer gets a caddying job at the golf club for tourists at Ingonish, fifteen miles away.

There's little for the older schoolboys of Neil's Harbour to do in the evenings but walk on the road and start going with girls. There's a card game and a dance now and then but not during Lent or the four weeks of Advent. There are no movies, no plays, no organizations; there's no place for a boy to go till he's twenty-one and allowed to visit the Legion Hall where he can play cards, throw darts, and drink beer.

"Freddie studies his spelling after supper while he walks around the kitchen, three or four trips around and it's all in his head," Jean says proudly. "He's always been good in school."

Children can go to grade eleven at Neil's Harbour's modern brick school; if they want their grade twelve, the Nova Scotia government pays forty dollars a month towards their board in Baddeck, ninety miles to the south. "We'd love to send our kids there but we couldn't afford it," Jean laments. "They'd need better clothes and books and money to spend and to get there and back. The only hope we have of giving them an education is if they went into the armed services and took a course. Fifteen young ones from around here are in now."

Freddie's head appears round the door as he says, "Get supper, mom."

And Jean adds, "I'll hate to see that kid go but I know that some day I got to."

As she starts setting the table, Jean continues, "I don't know what's going to become of this place if all the young ones keep leaving it and the fishing ain't better. I try to live one day at a time and not think of what's coming but Owen worries about it. He thinks he might have to leave us and try for a job on a big boat somewhere. He'd be gone then for maybe months at a time and I don't know how we'd live without him, he's so good with the kids and never leaves me at night." Jean stoops to fix her slipper, which doesn't need fixing, but the movement hides her quick tears.

"I wouldn't ever want to go away from here and live some other place. No one that ever left the Harbour would have done it if they could have made a living here. I couldn't content myself to live nowhere else. So long as we're all alive and warm and well fed, I'm happy here."

Chatelaine, December, 1961

Jean and Owen still live in their little house in Neil's Harbour. Beth, their sixth child, is the only one left at home. "We miss all the others," Jean says, "but they aren't far away and come back whenever they can."

Jean isn't working so hard now; during the lean years she got a job as cook's assistant at the little Red Cross hospital so Freddie was able to go to the high school in Baddeck, then to university in Halifax, then teacher's college and library school.

In the meantime, two miles from Neil's Harbour,

John Cabot High School was built to serve Cape Breton's north shore. Freddie is the head of its English department and library. He collects and keeps Cape Breton archives and last summer received a Canada Council grant to go to England to study the origins of non-Gaelic Cape Bretonners. He has a wife and two sons. When I asked him what had happened to his Neil's Harbour accent, he grinned and said, "It comes back whenever I'm out in the boat with my dad."

Wilbert Williams too went to university; he became a chartered accountant in Halifax. Donna went to business school, married a boy in Smelt Brook, had three children, and now works in the office of the fish company in Neil's Harbour. Yvonne went to university and Miss Murphy's School for Young Ladies in Halifax; the last time I visited, she was travelling abroad with her husband. Her Aunt Martie told me, "Yvonne talks lovely now and looks so smart." Norman went into the navy for a while and now is back at the fishing. Beth, in her last year at John Cabot, plans to become an anthropologist.

Since the two-hundred-mile limit was declared, inshore fishing has improved. Jean and Owen enjoy more comforts than they'd ever dreamed of. Owen has a bigger boat (not quite paid for), which he keeps in the harbour at Dingwall, running back and forth in his own pick-up truck. Jean smiles happily. "Fishin' still ain't that good but we always keep hoping."

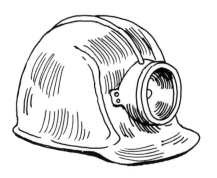

Miner's Wife

*I*n 1961, *Chatelaine* sent me to the iron-mining
town of Wawa to write about the family of a miner
who drills and blasts two thousand feet underground.
Via Algoma Central Railway, I arrived during the
spring fishing and blackfly season. There were no
motels, the only hotel was filled with sports
fishermen, but the manager sent me to the home of a
miner whose wife drove me from one miner's small
house to another until we found a family that had a
spare bed in their basement and would let me live
with them for a week or two.

"My heart's in my mouth all the time Porky's working down in the mine," says Rose Wheatley. "I'm always afraid he's been killed and I'm a widow with three little children."

Porky puts his hand on her shoulder. "Honey, you get too excited. No one's been killed in our mine since last year."

Rose smiles dubiously at her husband's assurance; she is happy and confident only when he is safely beside her.

Rose and Gordon (Porky) Wheatley live in Wawa, Ontario, an iron-mining town on the new link of the Trans-Canada Highway around Lake Superior, one hundred sixty miles north of Sault Ste. Marie. Porky, a miner, drills and blasts rock two thousand feet underground, while Rose worries and wishes he could do something safer and easier. "But how else could he make such a good living?" she asks wistfully as she glances at her automatic washing machine, dryer, and freezer.

Rose is a striking, black-haired woman of twenty-nine, with a figure a model might envy. She is generous and friendly; she loves pretty clothes, a clean house, and someone to talk to. With the fire of a volatile temperament inherited from parents who came out from Italy, she disciplines her beautiful children, Lynn, nine, Lee, seven, and Lou, six, and works like a mad thing to dispel her anxiety while Porky is down in the mine.

Porky, whose prickly crew-cut hair accounts for his nickname, is quiet and calm, with a muscular, slim-hipped physique developed by weight-lifting, boxing, and work. He likes to play poker, to go fishing, and moose hunting, but each working day he dutifully leaves the security of sunlight and sinks down into the darkness that is dripping and cold, the air thick with stone dust and blasting smoke. He wears a hard helmet with a light on the front, shatter-proof glasses, rubber trousers and jacket, steel-toed boots, and heavy gloves. He uses a grease-spattering rock drill that is gradually making him deaf, and dynamite that could blow him to bits if he's careless.

"I nearly go crazy when Porky's late getting home from the mine." The dark circles round Rose's eyes come from long nights of waiting. "It seems like I'm holding my breath till he comes in the door."

Porky smiles gently – a smile that is slightly shame-faced – as he explains the traditional compensation of miners. "When a man's been underground for eight hours he's so glad to see daylight again that he feels he's just got to go in for a beer."

"Porky doesn't do it too often," Rose defends him. "In his spare time he mostly works around home, or helps out a neighbour, or does things with me and the kids. We love living in Wawa but I sure wish Porky never had to go down the shaft."

Porky says, "The only thing that scares me is a lay-off."

"Do you think there might be one?" Rose is quickly alarmed.

"There's plenty of ore but you can't control economic conditions. I'm not trained for any other job and we seem to need more than the seven thousand dollars or so that I'm earning in a year."

"The Buick and dryer and freezer are paid for," Rose says.

"But we must add more rooms to the house."

Civilization has caught up with the Canadian miner. He is no longer just an escapee from city life or a love affair, an adventurer who fled to the hinterland to seek his fortune in mining. Today he is a man who settles down with a family, has a high standard of living, and belongs to a union. Mining is rapidly becoming just another heavy industry. It no longer requires the brute strength of huge men who used picks and shovels, lived in bunkhouses, drank hard, fought like animals, made money, lost it, and moved on. Now mucking machinery and fast-drilling equipment make it possible for a lithe, intelligent man like Porky Wheatley to outwork several old-time giants.

Porky graduated from high school in his native Saskatchewan. Though not qualified, he taught for a term in a prairie school, then came to Wawa and for ten years has worked in the mine, where he has become a development miner, whose job is to make tunnels in the rock and ore-body by drilling holes, filling them with dynamite, blasting, and mucking up the resulting debris. On an incentive system of payment, he is one of the highest-paid underground workers of Algoma Ore Properties, a division of Algoma Steel, commonly known in Wawa as "the Company."

Without the Company, Wawa probably wouldn't exist.

Almost one quarter of its 4,196 inhabitants is on the Company's payroll, working in the fifty miles of tunnels that comprise its two underground iron mines, or in its open-pit mine, in offices, or in the sinter plant, where the ore is prepared for use in the steel mills. When the Company started mining hematite iron in 1898, Wawa became a boom town (with a hotel that had a bar a foot higher than standard so the miners couldn't jump over it to grab bottles or fight with the bartender). Twenty years later the mine closed and Wawa was a ghost town. Before the Second World War, the company again operated its surface siderite mines and Wawa revived. In 1950 the company decided to mine the millions of tons of iron that were underground, and the enormous expansion that followed brought many workers to Wawa. Rose Wheatley's father, a miner, moved over from Timmins. Rose came to look for a job, met Porky – also newly arrived – and six months later they were married.

Houses were scarce in Wawa; the miners cleared land of dense forest and built their own homes. Porky built his like all the others, set on cement blocks without a foundation, with asbestos-shingle exterior and Gyproc walls and ceilings. When he finished his own house he helped his neighbours build theirs. What had they to lose, they asked themselves. If the mine lasted they would make money, stay a few years, then move on. When the minister of the United Church, which served all denominations but Anglican and Roman Catholic, wanted to establish a Protestant cemetery, people said, "Why should we bother? We won't stay long enough to die here."

Like Rose and Porky, most of the people in Wawa were not yet thirty years old. There was no way for them to get out of town to have fun except by the Algoma Central Railway to the Sault, and the trip was too long to make in a weekend. They amused themselves with fishing and hunting, dancing, gambling, talking, or drinking. Porky played poker and hockey; Rose had three babies in rapid succession. They saved money to buy a car, which they couldn't drive farther than a few miles through the bush.

In 1955 the Company spent millions of dollars on further expansion and Wawa took on an aspect of permanency. There had always been a great turnover of men but now those who were there settled down. Seventy per cent of the miners were men from Europe who had been displaced by the war. They longed for security, for roots in their new land, and for a place to bring up their children. They worked hard, fenced in their properties, and dug basements under their houses. Native Canadians who had built their own homes changed their minds about leaving them.

Under his house, Porky Wheatley dug, shovelful by shovelful, an area thirty feet square, nine feet deep. Propping the building on timbers, he laid a cement-block foundation and cemented the floor. The resulting enclosure is now one of the most used rooms in the house. In one corner is a round table where every week Porky and his pals play poker all Friday night and all day Saturday. In another corner there is a bed, where I slept while I stayed with the Wheatleys. Along one wall are the freezer, shelves of canned goods, laundry equipment, and a cupboard for dishes to be used when there is a party. A play area for the children is near the steep stairway that leads to the tiny entryway of the house.

The first room one enters on the main floor is the blue-and-white kitchen, where there is always activity: Lou playing with a toy, Porky making a Western sandwich on the large electric stove, neighbours sitting at the Arborite table having coffee with Rose, who seldom drinks more than half of hers because she must answer the telephone, fill Porky's lunch pail, brush Lynn's and Lee's pony tails, or do six dozen other things.

At the front of the house is the living room, with a stained-plywood dado and walls painted turquoise. It is furnished with a new chesterfield suite, Rose's desk-model sewing machine, and a coffee table on which there are piles of magazines: *Chatelaine*, *True Love*, and *Muscles*. A combination radio and record player constantly blares hit tunes of the day. On top of the valance board over the picture window are trophies that Porky has won for boxing, bowling, dart-throwing, and silently sitting among them is Polly, the budgie, who looks down her beak at the humans beneath her.

Adjoining the living room is Rose's and Porky's bedroom, and behind it a narrow room where the three children sleep in bunk beds – Lou on the lower, the two girls above. "Their dresses and crinolines are stuffed so tight in their closet that I have to press them before they can wear them," Rose complains. Porky consoles her: "Some day we'll add two bedrooms where we now have our driveway."

Though boundless wilderness surrounds Wawa, its houses are huddled together on fifty-foot lots covered with gravel, except for a few nurtured lawns. Rose says, "I'd love to have enough topsoil brought in so we could plant grass and radishes and a flower or two, but sometimes the fumes from the Company sinter plant blow down on this end of town and everything withers away."

There are few trees along Wawa's streets; the sunshine is so precious that no one wants shade. Temperatures drop to forty degrees below zero in winter. When spring comes, late in May, cold winds still sweep down the hills. The summers are cool with sudden hot days that are too infrequent to kill the mosquitoes and blackflies that plague people all through the season.

Wawa is stark but it is surrounded by beauty. To the north are the high rocky hills of the Michipicoten Range, with the plum-coloured smoke from the sinter plant rising above them. Behind the main street is Wawa Lake, named by the Indians for the wild geese that rest there in migration. Nearby is Lake Superior, with its white beaches, where the Wheatleys scoop up smelts in the spring and in summer go boating and swimming. Innumerable trout streams and small lakes abound in the area, and the forest of evergreen and birch comes into the back yards along the outer streets of the town. "We might see a moose from our kitchen window," Rose says, "and bears have come out and knocked over our garbage."

Thousands of hunters, fishermen, and tourists have been passing through Wawa since the new highway around Lake Superior was opened in September 1960. They give the town an air of bustle and promise. Several motels are being built, and to cash in on the new influx of visitors, many Wawa families are putting beds in their basements and renting rooms for the night. The Ace, a new Chinese restaurant, serves twenty-four hours a day. Rose loves nothing better than to go there for coffee and to see who's around.

The new highway has given the citizens of Wawa access to the world; they don't feel shut in any more, because they now can drive to the Sault in a few hours. Rose and Porky sometimes get a sitter to stay with the children and run down for a weekend of shopping and night clubs on the American side. Until she came to Wawa, Rose hadn't been farther from her home in Timmins than nearby Noranda. In the last year they have visited Rose's father, a miner in Steep Rock, one hundred miles west of Port Arthur, and have driven to Toronto and Stratford, an exciting experience for the children, who had never seen cows, and for Rose, who saw her first willow tree.

"It's good to get out and see how other people live," Rose tells her friends. "And you should see the difference in prices! We pay far more for things in Wawa than they do in any places we've been. That blue dress I bought for sixteen dollars was only ten in Toronto. We pay thirty-two cents for milk and they pay twenty-three."

Rose loves to go downtown to look around for bargains. Broadway, the main street of Wawa, is paved and has cement walks and stores on both sides – two well-stocked, modern supermarkets, a gift shop, a new Hudson's Bay Company store, several dress shops that satisfy Rose's fashionable taste, and a drug store where she buys fascinating shades of eye shadow, nail polish, and lipstick.

Almost everyone she meets in Wawa calls, "Hi, Rose," and many stop for a chat. People know Rose because she is on the Wawa Ladies' Softball Team, is secretary of the Bowling League, and teaches at the United Church Sunday school. On pay night she and Porky go with friends to the Rose Room of the Wawa Hotel for cocktails and to listen to the electric organ. On Saturday nights they attend dances at the Union Hall, and every other week, while Porky is on night shift, a teenager stays with the Wheatley children and Rose sells tickets at the Roxy, Wawa's movie theatre.

"I love working at the show," Rose says. "I like to dress up and meet people; it gets me out of the rut of just being a housewife. I'm through at nine-thirty; then I go home and scrub floors with the radio going full blast, or I make clothes for the kids because there's nobody around to bother me.

Sometimes I take my ironing next door to Pat MacRae's and watch TV with her. I often wait up for Porky – I can't sleep when he's underground, and anyway it's nicer for him coming in at four in the morning. I make him some soup and a snack. Then we go to bed, and he sleeps while I get the kids up for school."

Rose has no routine for her housework. She's likely to be doing her washing any day of the week at two in the morning or at three in the afternoon. When Porky's on day shift they get up at six, and if she doesn't go back to bed until eight, her house is shining and neat before nine. Some days she never stops working. Other days she makes a tour of the neighbourhood, drinking coffee with friends; or they come to her kitchen to chat.

"Those are nice elastic pants, Rose," Doreen Hogean says of the "slim jims" Rose is wearing.

"They're old. I always wear old clothes to work in. It's when I go out I like to really dress up." Rose stops polishing the floor to show Doreen the tiara, silver eye shadow, and new organza evening dress she has bought. "I never had more than one dress at a time when I was a kid," Rose says. "We were so poor. That's why I crave things like this to make up for it. And Porky likes me to look nice. But I can't save any money."

Lynn and Lee come in from school. Lynn has blue eyes fringed with long black lashes; Lee's eyes are dark and enquiring. Dainty jewelled earrings dangle from their pierced ears. They are wearing bright-yellow slickers, flowered kerchiefs, and little red nylon gloves.

"Look at the outfits they've put on," Rose exclaims. "Kids seem to have no idea about what goes together. I'm trying to teach them." She passes the handle of the electric floor polisher to Lee. "Start in the hall. Lynn, tidy your room." To Doreen she says, "They've both got regular jobs to do every day. I don't want them to get married and not know how to keep house."

"That'll be a while yet, won't it? They're just seven and nine."

Rose agrees. "But it could happen in a few years, and the sooner the better as far as I'm concerned. I'm looking forward

more to being a grandmother than anything else in my life."
Rose sits at the table for a moment and sips at her coffee. "If
only they don't get husbands too far from Wawa."

Lou, rosy and sturdy, comes in from playing. "Mom, can I
have a cookie?"

"No, my son." Rose glances at the clock on the wall. "It's
near five o'clock and time for me to make supper."

Rose flies around her kitchen when she's cooking. She
makes pudding, date squares, and banana bread, meat balls,
rigatoni, macaroni, chicken or spare ribs baked in the oven
with olive oil, onions, bay leaves, and garlic. Two or three
times a week she makes a great pot of spaghetti; she serves it
to friends who come in for an evening or after a dance.

Joyce and Bill Boychuk, the Hogeans, the MacRaes, or the
Pollards – the men all development miners – often drop in to
talk about various things. They discuss the difficulties of do-
it-yourself work in their houses; they say they make mistakes
that cost money. Porky points out a corner of the living room
where the squares don't quite meet.

Bill Boychuk and Porky talk about their last game of poker.
"You work so hard for your money in the mine and when you
come out and get into a poker game you might make as much
money just playing," Porky says.

Bill agrees. "You can be lucky and win more in one night
than you earn in two weeks of hard slugging underground."

"But with a family I guess you couldn't count on making
your living that way," Porky muses, and idly shuffles the
cards he carries around in his pocket. "I often look at that old
derelict miner who hangs around town, in and out of poker
games for years, drinking and playing. Makes you wonder
where you're going and if it's worthwhile."

"What can you be sure of these days?" Bill asks.

The miners are always afraid of a lay-off. They mention
Elliot Lake, ghost towns, and the early history of Wawa. They
don't say "If the mine fails," only "If there's a lay-off, what
will we do?" They agree that they are paid well, but they spend
what they make; they are used to their standard of living and
wouldn't want less. They say development mining is interesting work but there's no future in it. When urged by their

wives, they agree that if they could make as much money out of the shaft as in it they would come out. But what else can a man do who is trained for nothing but mining? they ask.

"I often thought about going into some kind of business," Porky says, "but I wouldn't know what."

"We'll have to come out of the mine some day. Do you know any underground drillers over forty-five years old?"

"You can stand it for only so long."

"The vibration gets you, or you get rheumatism from the dampness and cold."

"Or silicosis from stone dust, though they say our mine's not too bad for that."

"I just hope our kids are smart enough to get more education and do something else."

"I'd like mine to be teachers, or to marry teachers," Rose says. "That's what I'd have been if my mother wouldn't have had to scrub floors to keep me in school. But Lynn and Lee want to be ballet dancers. They can't learn that in Wawa."

There is no vocational training at the new Wawa high school; home economics, commercial work, and manual training are not taught. Most children drop out without finishing their matriculation; there are seventy pupils in grade nine, only five in grade thirteen. There's not much for girls to do in Wawa but work in a store or a restaurant, the hotel, or the hospital. They marry early. The boys go to the mine, where there are fifty distinctly different operations to be done underground.

It takes two years for a good worker to become a development miner, who has perhaps the most dangerous, most difficult (though best-paying) miner's job. Rose thinks it must also be the dirtiest. "Porky's doeskin shirts and long woollen underwear are so heavy with grease from the drill," she says, "that I can't get them clean. They just fall apart if they're washed, so he throws them away."

"Hogean's are the same, and every week he wears out a pair of rubber gloves that cost a dollar and a quarter," says Doreen when the miners' wives gather in Rose's kitchen.

"Lorne's on graveyard this week," says Marie Pauli of her fiancé. The graveyard shift is from eleven-thirty at night till seven in the morning.

"Don't you hate that?" asks Doreen. "All the accidents seem to happen at night. If Wawa mines weren't supposed to be the safest in the country I wouldn't let Hogean go underground. But still I'm nervous and I can never get to sleep till he's home."

"I guess you never get over it. My mum didn't." Rose's father has been mining for thirty years. "Porky says there's only been five killed in the ten years we've been here. If it does happen they say it's their own fault because safety regulations are so strict."

"Yeah, they get the axe if they're caught cutting corners to speed up their work and increase their bonus."

"Porky got his arm caught one time when he was up in a raise [a vertical tunnel]. He hollered and they came up and got him, but if the holes he'd been drilling hadn't gone through so they could hear him, he might have been up there for hours."

"I'd like to go down the mine sometime," says Marie.

"I wouldn't," Doreen declares emphatically. "It's bad enough thinking about what Hogean has to do down there without going and seeing it. Standing in the wet mud with water dripping on them through the rock, and so dark." She shudders.

"Porky says it's black dark, nothing could be darker and nothing is louder than drilling and blasting."

"Smokey's getting real deaf," Pat puts in quietly.

"Sometimes when Porky comes home it's almost an hour before he can hear me." Rose laughs. "And you know how I yell."

"Fred says the air is thick as fog with dust and blasting smoke. I guess they really need to go into the bush to get healthy air in their lungs."

"That's what they always say, anyway, when they leave you home alone for a weekend."

Rose feeds her friends spaghetti round her kitchen table at midnight before they go home to wait for their men.

"You moved your table and fridge again, Rose," Joyce Pollard observes. "How come?"

"Last night I was nervous," Rose says. "I had a feeling there was something wrong in the mine. When I get that way I have to pitch in and do something or I'll go crazy." She crooks her fingers tensely. "I took the bunk beds apart in the kids' room and carried them into the basement. I dragged down the mattresses and springs, then the girls' chest of drawers. I carried the bed from the basement and set it up where the bunks were, put Lou in it, waxed and polished the floor, took all the girls' clothes from the closet to the rack in the cellar, swept and scrubbed the linoleum down there, and put the girls into bed."

"How could you do all that?" asks Marie. "I'd be dead."

Rose shrugs her shoulders. "I just knew there was trouble underground. By four in the morning I'd switched the refrigerator and the table and chairs in the kitchen, finished my ironing, and cleaned the kitchen cupboards.

"I made soup for Porky, thinking he'd be home any minute. But he didn't show up. Quarter past four and he wasn't home yet. Four-thirty, half an hour late. By then I was sure he was dead. I sat by the phone and waited for someone to tell me.

"At twenty to five he came in. He'd been having coffee at the Ace." Rose clutches a handful of hair on the top of her head. "I could have murdered him – till he told me that two men had been hurt when they fell from a ladder in one of the raises, legs and arms and ribs broken. Wasn't it awful? Porky said if the raise hadn't been at an angle they would have been killed."

"Better killed falling down a raise than being blown up like that fellow last year. They only found forty pounds of him scattered around."

"Oh, don't, I can't stand it." Marie Pauli puts her hands over her face.

"You got to face it, if you're going to marry a miner."

"Men get killed other ways too. They're safer down in the mine than they are driving around in a car."

"Yeah, that's what they always tell us," Rose says. "And yet, you know, no matter how much I worry, I'd rather be married to Porky and live here in Wawa than do anything else I can think of."

Chatelaine, March, 1962

☆   ☆   ☆   ☆   ☆

Throughout twenty years Christmas greetings came to me from the Wheatleys.

On my return from a motor trip to British Columbia in 1976, I stayed overnight in Wawa. Except for the number of fine new motels and a few more small stores, the town seemed to have changed very little since 1961.

I invited the Wheatleys to have dinner with me at a restaurant that had succeeded the Ace. Rose, glamorous as ever, had become the manager of Sear's mail-order office. Porky, quite deaf and no longer able to work underground, had just come out of a three-and-a-half-month stay in hospital, suffering acutely from arthritis.

In a recent phone conversation with Rose I was told that conditions in Wawa are grim now. "But I guess they are bad everywhere," Rose said. "The mine is only open half time: the men are on one week and off the next."

"Are you still working at Sear's?"

"Oh yes, full time. And you know I'm a grandmother now; Lee has three children. But they live in Sault Ste. Marie and we don't see them as often as we'd like to.

"What about Lynn and Lou?" I asked her.

"Lynn's been working at the hardware store for over five years; she got married in December to a miner, a really talented man, who can fix cars and do carpentry too. Lou was in the army for four years; he's living in Winnipeg now, taking courses and looking for work. He likes it out west."

"And Porky, what about Porky? Lynn wrote me that he retired before he was fifty because of his arthritis."

"Yes, he's home all the time now, has good and bad days. He does leather and bead work to keep from being bored."

"Does he still play cards?"

"Oh yeah, but not those twenty-four-hour games like he used to. Just a minute." Rose left the phone and quickly returned. "Porky wants me to tell you he shot a deer last week and he's canning the venison. Week before last he canned a moose."

"Fabulous!" I said. "And are you still serving spaghetti to all your friends?"

Rose laughed. "We always have plenty of that, but I don't make it as spicy as I used to, I've got a bleeding ulcer. We have to go down to the Sault regularly to have check-ups at the doctor's but we don't mind that because then we can see our grandchildren; they're ten, seven, and five, and they are beautiful."

We're Happy Being Slaves
of Jehovah

*I*n the summer of 1963, John Clair, editor of the
Toronto Star's weekly magazine, asked me to go to
a Jehovah's Witness conference in Hamilton,
Ontario, to find out why they persist in
proselytizing, why they refuse blood transfusions,
what they think about life after death, and why
Jehovah's Witnesses claim to be the world's fastest
growing religion.

Because Witnesses who came to my door were
sometimes a nuisance and hard to get rid of, and
those who stood on street corners holding up their
magazines, *Watchtower* and *Awake*, often looked
sadly pathetic, I accepted the assignment without
much enthusiasm. But soon I learned to respect the
many Witnesses I met as trusting, sincere, friendly
people.

A few days before Jehovah's Witnesses gathered at a district conference in Hamilton, Ontario's civic stadium last summer, seventeen hundred of them came from miles around with pails, brushes, and detergents; in an hour they had scrubbed all the benches, posts, floors, and lavatories of the great concrete structure – and had a jolly time doing it.

Witnesses say no task is too menial to perform for God's kingdom. They call themselves slaves of Jehovah and will gladly do anything commanded in the Bible – as it is translated and interpreted by the leaders of their sect.

They believe that people who are busy have no time to get into mischief. Witnesses are constantly reading and quoting their Bibles, going to meetings, and giving free time and labour to assemblies and to their society's building projects.

Probably no other religious cult in the world works so persistently at spreading its message. In sun, rain, or snow, Jehovah's Witnesses stand for hours on street corners selling *Awake!* and *Watchtower*, their religious magazines; every week they trudge from door to door offering their publications and their beliefs to people they hope to bring into their fold. Last year in Canada forty-one thousand Witnesses spent five million hours preaching and ringing the doorbells of fellow Canadians.

To find out what these people really are like, what they believe, and why they insist on bothering other people with their proselytizing, I spent a weekend at their assembly in Hamilton, attended meetings in their Kingdom Hall in Kitchener, and went to Bible-study groups in one of their homes.

I approached the conference with reluctance, expecting a noxious display of hysterical evangelism.

I found more than fourteen thousand Witnesses, adults and children, sitting submissively on the backless benches of the stadium in the hot August sun, listening with quiet dignity from nine o'clock in the morning till nine at night to academic, unemotional, monotonous speeches being read by their leaders over loudspeakers that boomed from a platform in the playing field, artistically banked with flowers.

Except for a larger number of Negroes among them than one usually encounters in a crowd of Canadians (the Hamilton Witness district includes part of New York State), the

Witnesses looked like any modestly dressed group of people, more young than old. Most of them carried Bibles and hymn books, cushions, or cameras, which they trustingly left on their seats to reserve their places between sessions. During these intermissions they patiently made their way to the area under the concrete bleachers where they ate and joyfully greeted their friends at this great inspirational event for which they'd been saving their pennies all year.

The conference was flawlessly organized, following the exact pattern set at Witness headquarters in Brooklyn, New York, for all assemblies held in the various districts in Canada, from Nanaimo to Moncton, and throughout the world. Seven hundred Witnesses had rung doorbells in Hamilton to find billets for over night guests. Booths were set up in the stadium to sell snacks, Bibles, and *Watchtower* magazines. There were booths to register Witnesses who wanted baptism, or accommodation, or to volunteer their help at the conference. Hot meals were served three times a day to fourteen thousand people standing at trestle tables. There was no disorder or litter. There was no solicitation of money.

The sessions were perfectly timed – as they easily could be, since the speeches had all been written at the sect's Brooklyn headquarters and were being delivered by men whose measured diction might have been learned at the same school of voice culture.

Witnesses listened spellbound as the truth was interpreted for them. They were given the Greek derivation of biblical words. They were told that since throughout history there have been many gods, the true God is distinguished by His personal Hebrew name of Jehovah. One speaker said Witnesses should marry only Witnesses, and wives were advised to subject themselves to their husbands. Children were urged to obey their parents and not fritter away their lives at public dances, sports events, or places of entertainment. "Plan your homework so you can attend five Witness meetings a week," they were told. "If higher education takes too much of your time, give it up and work for Jehovah." Smoking, they were told, was unclean; drinking in moderation, and card-playing for fun, were not forbidden.

Witnesses were warned that, while they may lawfully kill

and eat the flesh of beasts, fowl, and fish (being careful about certain brands of wieners and processed cold meats), they must not eat the blood thereof, according to Genesis; allowing blood to enter their veins by transfusion was interpreted as eating it. That is God's law, they were reminded, and if they transgress it, or allow their children to be given transfusions, they will sacrifice their right to eternal life. Glen How, a lawyer and ardent Witness from Toronto, informed me that the newspapers like to work up emotional hysteria about poor little Witness children being allowed to die without transfusions, but that actually many more people – according to recent medical reports – have died as a result of receiving contaminated blood or from human errors in giving transfusions.

From a medical standpoint, says How, there are two risks: "First, the patient may refuse a transfusion that could help him; secondly, he may accept a blood transfusion that would harm or kill him. When it is a matter of choice between the two, the patient or parent, as the case may be, must decide which to accept. The only time public officials can properly interfere is when the parents procure no skilled assistance and therefore are making no decision at all. This is abandonment of care of the child. But when parents, conscious of their responsibility, make a decision as to which risk they will accept, it is an abuse of official power to substitute the opinion of public officials for that of the parents."

One Witness at the Hamilton conference, a mother, told me, "I'd hate to be put to the test, but if I were, I'd choose temporary death for my child rather than lose him for all the years of eternity when I could have him well and happy beside me."

Most frequently stressed by the speakers at the conference was the need to search diligently for the sheep-like people of the world and to care for them; no fewer than ten hours a month should be spent by each Witness in door-to-door preaching and selling of Watchtower publications. "Push yourself a little," they were urged. "Never let secular employment keep you from doing Jehovah's work; if your job interferes, give up your job and have enough faith to expect a better job will turn up."

A fine example of such devotion, I was told, was that of the conductor of the assembly's volunteer orchestra and choir, a young German immigrant who had given up his musical career and become an accountant because the night work of his profession gave him little time for meetings and preaching; his wife, a ballet dancer, had stopped dancing so she could also work for the kingdom.

The reason for this urgency to spread their message was explained. Of all the people now living, Witnesses alone will enjoy life forever on earth; it is therefore their duty to save for eternity as many non-believers as they possibly can by bringing them "into the truth."

The highest award that is possible to Jehovah's Witnesses, I learned, is not eternal earthly life: God has selected exactly 144,000 (Rev. 7:4) from among Christians to become spiritual kings and princes with Jesus in heaven. Most of those chosen ones are already dead (among them Paul and eleven apostles, all Witnesses to Jehovah); those still alive are known as "the remnant" and now number 12,714. All are identified: they are the directors on the governing board of the New World Society and other dedicated Witnesses throughout the world who will forgo the joy of living on earth with their families in order to join the heavenly ruling class – a status not envied by the others, who look forward to an earthly paradise.

One morning of the conference was devoted to baptism. After a dedication service, twenty-three men wearing bathing trunks and undershirts stood waist-deep in the water of Hamilton's municipal swimming pool; a scattering of spectators and news photographers waited expectantly. "I bet Patricia will be nervous," a teenager behind me said. "Her bathing suit has only one strap."

From dressing-room entrances the candidates for baptism trickled in. Pretty girls in smart, scanty suits went confidently down steps into the water where the men in the undershirts instructed them how to hold their noses and hang on with their hands while they immersed them completely by tipping them backwards. Shy, stout old women came up sputtering and clinging. Men and young boys were dunked with dispatch. One large, lone Negro woman, wearing a faded cotton dress and boudoir cap, emerged with a look of transfiguration. Nurses stood by and served coffee and colas. In an hour, 381 Witnesses had been baptized and ordained.

All baptized Jehovah's Witnesses are practising ministers. No matter what or how little their education, all may teach, preach, and claim the status of clergy. All are trained and fully committed to spreading their message. Those who work only in their spare time are called "publishers" of the truth; "pioneers" are those who devote all their time and are willing to be sent by the society to wherever in the world they are needed. None receive any pay. Only the men of the sect may baptize, take charge of funerals, and perform weddings (but in Canada, the government gives a marrying licence to only one Witness in an area).

The New World Society of Jehovah's Witnesses (the full name of the sect) is the fastest-growing religion in the world, I was told at the conference. They make a thousand converts a week. While other Christian denominations have failed to double their memberships in the past twenty years, Witnesses claim an increase of 1,486 per cent. They have almost one million ministers zealously preaching in 185 lands and in 146 languages – more, Witnesses boast, than the number of Roman Catholic priests in the world, and several times the number of Protestant clergy. In Canada one person in every 443 is a Jehovah's Witness; in the United States, one in 635; in Northern Rhodesia, one in 82. The world membership of the society is 989,192. Only those who are publishing are enumerated in their statistics; small children and adherents are not counted as members.

At the last session of the conference there was a record attendance to hear the speech of Eugene D. Rosam, Jr., a thirty-five-year-old Floridian living in Toronto who is the superindendent of ministers for Canada. Witnesses listened with rapt attention as he told them that they need have no fear of nuclear war. They might actually anticipate it with pleasure, because it would bring about Armageddon in this generation: and the sooner the better, since witnesses will live joyfully ever after Armaggedon, the sole survivors of all now living on earth.

"Won't it be grand, sister?" a motherly, white-haired

woman said to me when the last speaker of the conference had finished. "I can hardly wait till Armageddon comes," she said, her sweet old face glowing. "I got a heart condition and I've been getting so tired. We live in the country where there aren't many Witnesses to do the Lord's work. It's hard tramping the roads and the lanes to bring people the message. Last week a woman set her dogs on me and my friend when we knocked at her door and we had to run through the fields." She smiled. "But the Bible says we've got to expect persecution for our faith, don't we, sister?"

Jehovah's Witnesses are proud of their martyrdom. During the First World War seven of their leaders in the United States were given twenty-year penitentiary terms for sedition (they were released in nine months). During the Second World War, Witnesses were tortured and gassed in Nazi concentration camps; in the United States more than seven thousand spent time in federal prisons for evading the draft. The sect was banned in Spain, Italy, Japan, and British Commonwealth countries, including Canada, where they carried on secretly, and where their young men were treated as conscientious objectors.

Witnesses declare they are aliens in all the world's countries. Though they obey the laws of the lands they inhabit, they express allegiance only to Jehovah God's kingdom and claim their rights as ambassadors. Wherever they live they won't vote, won't hold public office or participate in public affairs. As neutrals in international conflicts, they won't serve in military forces or salute any flag.

Pious and peace-loving Witnesses all over the world, no matter what their colour, customs, or nationality, affectionately call one another "brother" and "sister." They say that above all they try to obey Christ's command to love God and their neighbours – even those who are not "in the truth" – and they want nothing more than to save unbelievers from annihilation.

The benign attitude that now prevails amongst Witnesses is quite different from the abusive one that existed in the earlier days of the sect's history. The followers of Charles Taze Russell, a successful haberdashery salesman from Pennsylvania who started the sect eighty years ago (and predicted that the world would end in 1914), preached that there was no hell, scoffed at the Trinity, and offended orthodox Christianity by denouncing the Catholic and Protestant clergy as tools of the devil. In the days of Russell's successor, Judge J. F. Rutherford of Missouri, Witnesses became fiery-eyed fanatics who damned non-believers and marched in front of churches during Sunday services with signs proclaiming, "Religion is a Snare and a Racket."

Watchtower publications that depicted priests with horns on their heads roused Quebec's Roman Catholics to fury. In 1946 Witnesses became victims of violence throughout the province; though they seldom fought back, they were constantly arrested for disturbing the peace or charged for distributing pamphlets denouncing the clergy. Quebec City banned all Witness literature from being distributed – until the Supreme Court of Canada ruled in favour of Witnesses in cases of sedition, censorship, and false arrest. Witnesses in the province of Quebec now hold rallies and enjoy freedom from persecution as they do throughout the rest of the country.

Nathan Homer Knorr, the president of the New World Society since Rutherford's death in 1944, has written that present-day witnesses have no fight with any person because of religious beliefs. They merely differ from all other religions. They don't believe in the United Nations, in communism, evolution, the immortality of the soul, the deity of Jesus, or the symbol of the Cross (they say Christ was impaled on a stake without a cross-bar). They ignore Christmas and Easter as pagan celebrations; the Sabbath, they say, is a Jewish observance that need not be honoured but is a good day for selling their magazines.

Every two weeks there is a world circulation of more than six million copies of the *Watchtower*, the society's official theological magazine, which is printed in sixty-four languages, and more than 3,500,000 copies of *Awake!*, which contains news and comment. About 250,000 of each are distributed twice a month in Canada. Witnesses buy their self-imposed quotas – about twelve copies of each issue – for three cents apiece and sell them for five cents. Bibles and books of doctrine are also printed and sold annually throughout the world (556,000 books are sold in Canada).

No collection plate is ever passed at meetings of Witnesses. They claim that voluntary contributions of members and the unsolicited donations of adherents make possible the world-wide work of the society. Each Kingdom Hall is financed by its own congregation, whose offerings are put into a wooden box hanging on a back wall. No one knows how much anyone gives. They claim their expenses are low because no minister receives a salary and because, when any building is done, Witnesses contribute their skill, time, and labour. The large building on Highway 401 in Toronto, where the *Watchtower* magazines for Canada are printed from plates made in Brooklyn, would have cost $1 million but was built for much less because Witnesses in various building trades donated their services. When the building was ready for plumbing, fifty to one hundred plumbers came from far and near; electricians, painters, carpenters, and plasterers were equally generous.

I went several times to a Kingdom Hall, a new, neat little building that serves two congregations which each has four hour-long meetings in a week. "When we get more than a hundred fifty we split into two congregations so we don't lose the personal touch," I was told.

A friendly fellowship pervaded the gatherings, where everyone had a place in the sun: lonely old women could find someone to talk to; children sat with their parents and took part in the services; anyone putting up a hand might be called on to answer a theological question; any male could preach a sermon.

At weekly meetings of the theocratic ministry school I heard Witnesses learning to express themselves publicly and with poise. Young boys got up on the platform and confidently preached eight-minute sermons, which were kindly criticized by a congregational servant. The women, not allowed to preach in church, made mock house calls on each other for practice. "Your persuasion was very good, Sister Arachuk," the critic encouraged.

I attended several Bible-study meetings in the home of Norman Elvy, a machine operator and assistant overseer of a Witness congregation in Kitchener. Besides Brother Elvy and his wife – whom he called "Sister Toots" – there were usually seven other people enjoying each others' company in the back living room of the tidy, small house: a handsome young married couple; the Elvy's daughter, Gloria Jean, fourteen, with two of her friends; Sister Dorothy, a happy-looking woman of perhaps forty, and Enos, an attractive Egyptian-born Jewish girl who boards with the Elvys because her family objects to her being a Witness.

The well-disciplined meeting started with Brother Elvy standing and praying; he is a slight, neat, grey-haired man whose blue eyes are kind. From the society publication they were currently studying he asked questions printed at the bottom of each page and got well-worded replies that were also taken from the book. Passages from the Bible, referred to in the text, were read and discussed in the light of the book's literal interpretation. There was always perfect agreement with what had been read. Precisely one hour after it started, the study ended with prayer, and the announcement that the group would gather again on Saturday and Sunday mornings at nine to go out to preach and sell magazines.

"The whole city is divided up into small sections and every Witness has certain streets he or she must cover three times a year," Sister Toots told me.

"Don't you feel nervy knocking on people's doors?" I asked.

"Oh, no." Brother Elvy laughed. "Every door is a challenge. You go up to it wondering what kind of people will open it and how they will treat you. Some of our new publishers are shy at first; they always go with an experienced one, but when you've been at it for more than twenty years, as I have, it's a real thrill. We meet so many interesting people."

"And we have the great satisfaction of knowing we're bringing them news of God's Kingdom, if they're willing to listen," Enos added.

"You might make calls for a month and get no interest; then you get one that makes up for all the door-slamming," Sister Dorothy said.

"If people buy a book or a magazine we call back again in a week or so," Brother Elvy went on. "We try to get them interested enough to have a home Bible study."

"Then we go once a week for an hour and study the Bible with one of our books, like we do here in our group," Sister

Toots told me. "I went to Sister Dorothy's place every week for three years before she came out to a meeting. I'd push Gloria Jean in her buggy through the snow."

Dorothy smiled. "Without Toots I wouldn't have made it. I was an Anglican and my husband is an R.C. He didn't want me to have anything to do with Jehovah's Witnesses. But I knew that this was the truth and I had to stick with it no matter what. He still won't come with me but he lets me go and he thinks I'm a much better person than I was. He even gave me an automatic washing machine because I don't spend his money on bingo."

"Do you keep track of your converts?" I asked.

"Not exactly, because you don't do it yourself; it's Jehovah God working through you," Toots answered. "Every Witness has a record at headquarters in Brooklyn. Everything we do for the Kingdom we mark on a card every week. It tells all about us: when we're baptized, how long we've been preaching, the number of hours we spend making calls, how many meetings, what we did at them, how many book sales."

"You can see why our religion is our whole life." Brother Elvy smiled happily. "We're so busy working at it that we don't have time to do anything else."

"We love God so much we desire only to please Him," Enos said reverently. "We're happy being slaves of Jehovah."

Toronto Star Weekly, June, 1963

Jehovah's Witnesses assure me that their numbers are ever increasing. In Canada, since 1962, their membership has risen from 41,000 to 73,812, one person in 323, in the United States, one in 375. World membership in 205 countries is now 2,477,608; twenty years ago it was less than one million. The Witness magazines, *Watchtower* and *Awake*, now sell for twenty cents each, and have a monthly distribution of 10,050,000 and 8,200,000.

Norman Elvy and his wife, Sister Toots, now live

in a trailer camp in Stratford, Ontario, and are still faithful and zealous in spreading the word of the Kingdom.

Though I live in a secluded place in the country where no salesmen come, Witnesses call on me frequently. We talk about many things, and if they don't try to proselytize, I give them a cup of tea.

One day one of them said, "Oh, Edna, you are so kind, we sincerely wish we could save you."

Italian Canadians

*T*hough there are thousands of Italians in Toronto, trying to find a family to live with was like trying to find a needle in a haystack! The M.P.P. for the area promised to find a family for me but I didn't hear from him again. A newspaper columnist said, "No problem, I'll find someone for you," but he didn't ever call me back. I went to the priest of the parish and two days later he came up with a family: the wife was working all day, the husband all night, and the children were at school. No way. Finally as I walked through the Italian community, I noticed "Rooms to Let" and "Boarders Wanted" signs in the windows of quite a few homes. I looked at several and knew I couldn't live in them or with the people who showed them to me.

In a house on Grace Street a neat and friendly young woman took me to the third floor of her tall, narrow triplex, to a tiny unheated attic room with a canvas camp cot, two coat hangers and a cracked window mended with adhesive tape. "You bring bedcovers and more furniture," she told me. "Use bathroom downstairs with other Italian family, very nice man, lady, and three kids. You think you like?" she asked wistfully.

I liked her and suggested that we have a chat. She took me down to her kitchen, poured me a glass of Mille Fiore Liqueur, and agreed to let me come every morning and stay until bedtime, when I would return each night to my room at the new Westbury Hotel, not far away.

A lda and Bruno Pilli cannot read this story though it is being written about them and their two children and the alien life they lead in Toronto, where they are among the estimated 330,000 Italians who have come to live in the city since the end of the Second World War.

Bruno can laboriously spell out a few words, but Alda has no compulsion to learn to read English and could get along without speaking it, as do most of the Italian immigrant women who don't go to work outside their homes. They live in Little Italy, a crowded section of the west side of Toronto where the shopkeepers are Italian and most of the products they sell are imported from Italy. Moving-picture theatres in the area show only Italian films; priests preach in Italian, and hardly an English word is spoken among the Italian men who gather on the sidewalks, or among the Italian women who chat on their shabby front stoops. By living among their own countrymen, they cling securely to their old ways and language, while their children at school quickly become Canadians.

Like many similar Italian immigrant parents, Alda and Bruno have little contact with English-speaking people. Bruno came to Canada from northern Italy six years ago, and for most of that time he has had a job as a labourer with a plumbing-and-heating firm that employs other Italians. Alda, who came to the country a year after her husband, spends most of her time at home with their children, seven-year-old Luigi and four-year-old Paulo.

Alda is a sensitive, friendly woman of thirty, slender and tall, with the poise of good manners. She likes everything to be proper and clean. "I get red in face when somebody come and see we live in such old, not-nice house," she says. "Every day I busy, busy, busy, to make look better, but no good." In their native Gramolazzo, near the city of Lucca, Alda was a fashionable dressmaker. She was so pretty, popular, and gay that one year she was chosen by the football team as Miss Sport of her village of one thousand people and she received gifts and publicity. In Canada she is a pale, unnoticed, hard-working housewife with golden-brown eyes that often are wistful and lonely – until the supreme moment of the day, when Bruno comes home from his job.

When Bruno enters a room it is charged with his energy. He takes off his jacket, rolls up his shirt sleeves, and his marvellous muscles burst forth. So does his laughter and robust, lively talk. He is thirty-two, five feet eight inches tall, thick-set, bronzed, and broad-shouldered, with curly brown hair, smiling eyes, and a dimple set deep in his chin. He says, "I want always in my living to be able to hold my head high." He works hard and loves people. He enjoys playing *scopa* and *bocce* (card and lawn-bowling games), but he stays home every evening to save money for a visit to Italy and to buy a small home for his family.

"It seem like Italian think only money, money, money," Bruno says. "Is wrong." He shakes his head vigorously. "Everything we do is for our children."

"We come to Canada with nothing and need much," Alda adds. "In Italy not so many married women get job like in Canada. Bruno no like me to leave Paulo and Luigi." Alda smiles fondly. "When Bruno say no, I do no." Bruno grins.

The Pillis never engage a babysitter. They don't go to movies, to church, parties, or dances. They go to no sports events or places of entertainment. Like many of the Italians who make up 16 per cent of Toronto's population, Alda and Bruno live a monotonous, toiling, self-sacrificing existence to be able to give their children the advantages of a Canadian education and the Canadian way of life.

Their son Luigi, a quick, bright boy, is almost aggressively Canadian, not from excessive patriotism – which, at seven, he could hardly understand – but because he wants to be just like the other boys at school. Paulo, a pale, blue-eyed child, imitates his older brother. Though Luigi is affectionate and has a sweet disposition, he is sometimes impatient when his parents can't remember the English words they have asked him to tell them.

"Stupid," he mutters, "stupid."

"Luigi say he no like Italian ways, no like Italian-style face," Alda tells me. "He no like short, dark Italian mans with black" – she rubs a finger over her upper lip to illustrate the word *moustache*, which she doesn't know in English. "Why is this?" she asks. "Why he so much want to be Canadian that he no like Italian?" Alda's wide eyes show distress. "I like Canada

213

but I love too my own country where I born. I not understand Luigi."

Alda's words express the tragedy of many immigrants who never can bridge the gap between their old culture and the new, while the children for whom they sacrifice adopt with ease ways that are strange to their parents and cause conflict as the family grows older if bonds of affection have not been carefully nurtured.

Alda and Bruno can't learn much of Canada while living in Little Italy, with its customs not unlike those of their homeland. They read no Canadian publications; they listen to no English-language radio programs, and seldom watch a TV show (Bruno says TV is for kids).

The Pillis live in a house that frustrates them. They pay $110 a month to rent the long, narrow, centre section of a triplex with nine rooms, and they live in two – a bedroom and kitchen on the main floor. They hoped to rent the rest of the house, to get cheaper rent, but the house is old and run-down and tenants don't stay very long.

When the Pillis moved in a year ago the second floor was rented by a family of Portuguese who were friendly but got up every morning at four and noisily fried fish for their breakfast. Bruno asked them to leave. A family of seven swarthy Sicilians moved in; a young couple lived with the Pillis, and a room in the attic was rented – so there were fourteen people living in the house. Then there was a lapse with no tenants. Now five Calabrians on the second floor are complaining that the plumbing is rotten.

On the main floor, the front room is occupied by Francesco Lutano, a kindly, middle-aged mechanic from Rome who boards with the Pillis, and says, "Miss Alda cooks very very nice."

The Pillis spend most of their time in their narrow, white-walled kitchen with a small refrigerator, a gas stove, and a stainless-steel sink. The room's only furniture is a formica-topped table and six padded chrome chairs; if the number of visitors and the family exceeds the number of seats, Alda and Bruno lead against the cupboard or hover over their guests serving coffee or wine and the children sit on the floor.

In the Pillis' small bedroom there is little space between the pieces of second-hand furniture except in front of a television set, placed where it can be seen through the kitchen doorway.

Another door from the kitchen leads outside and to the cellar where there is a toilet, shower, and laundry tubs in which, three times a week, Alda rubs dirty clothes on a washboard and is grateful for having hot water coming out of a tap. In earth on the floor of the basement, Alda grows *radic-chio*, a bitter-tasting plant brought out from her homeland. In the spring she transplants the bleached sprouts to the back yard where they grow quickly into long, dark leaves that can be cooked or eaten in salads. "Very good for the blood," Alda claims.

The Pillis' back yard is sixteen feet wide; a ramshackle garage, unsafe for use, leans crazily over the end of it. Predatory cats prowl along the board fences down both sides. In winter and spring Paulo plays there in the snow or the mud. In summer Alda and Bruno transform the sour-smelling earth to a garden by planting tomatoes, broccoli, and *radicchio*, with pansies and parsley bordering a narrow concrete path that leads to an alley. Beyond is the parking lot of a supermarket surrounded by the shabby backs of old houses and stores. From the small window of her kitchen-living-room that's all Alda can see.

When asked if she's happy in Canada, Alda sometimes smiles and says it is wonderful, but other times she shrugs and looks sad. "I love my husband and Luigi and Paulo," she says, "but that's all I got here. I miss very much my mommy and daddy and all friends I had in Italia."

"We had such nice house by the sea in Via Reggio on Riviera," Bruno tells me. "Many flowers all over, pine trees like big umbrella, carnival for much fun –"

"And place for dance," Alda interrupts. "I love Riviera." Her eyes brighten. "Night time is so *bella* when fishing boats go with lights on the water, and every day I take Luigi for walk on promenade with stylish tourists to look at and people I know." Alda sighs and quickly bends her head as she sweeps the kitchen floor for the third time in the day with a fibre broom from Venice.

"In Italy before I marry I no do hard work, no washing, no scrub. My family is good medium family, not poor, not rich;

my brother go long to school and is now electric engineer in Genoa."

Alda and Bruno went to school till they were eleven, the compulsory age-limit for free education in Italy. "From when I am fourteen I love Bruno," Alda smiles. "Much other boy want me but I want only him; Bruno see lots girl but only want me. We marry when I have twenty-one year."

Bruno drove a transport truck through the narrow streets of Italian cities, where there were no speed limits, through snow-covered mountains with dangerous passes and many hair-pin turns. He was away from home for weeks at a time and the strain of his work made him nervous.

"Bruno made eighty thousand lire [about $130] a month," Alda tells me. "Is not bad, but I cry, cry, when Bruno is all the time gone. If Bruno didn't drive truck he would be just labourer and that is very poor in Italia. No future for Luigi – then baby. So Bruno think he come to Canada and try for maybe a year. People tell us money jump in the pockets over here."

Bruno laughs. "I soon find it only jump out."

Bruno came alone to Canada, knowing no one and speaking no English. He was sent to Regina where he worked for very low pay. He cut lumber in British Columbia till he realized he was doing harder work for less money than English-speaking newcomers on the job. He moved to Toronto and worked in a garage for eight-five cents an hour till he got the labourer's job he has now with the plumbing-and-heating firm. It pays him $2.05 an hour – about four thousand dollars a year if there isn't a lay-off.

"Boss I got is very good guy," Bruno says, "and I belong to labour union. I like to learn to be plumber, but can't get so much pay while learning – I couldn't afford. Alda and kids get often sick. Paulo have tonsil off and we pay much for doctor."

"First year here I sick in hospital," Alda says. "I cry, cry, all the time homesick for my country. I bring just clothes and bed-covers because Bruno say we stay only four or five year. I have everything still in Italia: many presents from wedding, silver, champagne glass, my nice house. For this I cry." Tears are not far from Alda's eyes as she speaks. "Then Paulo born and I stop. Much to do for baby."

216

Alda is a compulsive worker. In her two rooms everything must be spotless. She scrubs walls, sews, cooks, and every day shops for food as she did in Italy. She says, "I like everything to be fresh."

There are many Italian food stores just round the corner from the Pillis' that make Alda feel quite at home. Several have ripe and green olives in barrels of brine. Italian butcher shops have gutted kids and fleecy black lambs hanging in their windows with salami and mortadella sausages. At the Violante Groceteria Alda buys fresh anise, rapini, artichokes, and oregano. At the Vesuvio Bakery she buys Paulo a cone of spumone or selects fancy Italian cakes with cheese fillings, coloured icings, and pistachios.

In Johnnie Lombardi's Supermarket she enters a door marked ENTRATA, passes spaghetti and espresso coffee-makers, shelves of packaged pasta in innumerable forms, jars of piccalilli and peperoncini. Hanging from bars near the ceiling she sees great provolini cheeses and prosciutto – Italian cured ham that sells for $3 a pound. At the record bar she hears a hit tune sung by Luciano Tajoli, "the song-bird of Italy."

Alda says she likes living in a big city; there are many people to look at and she enjoys window-shopping. For several blocks along College Street between Bathurst and Shaw, men, accustomed to gathering in the outdoor cafés and in the sunny flowering plazas of Italy, stand in groups along the bleak sidewalks to chat. Alda passes them by as she studies window displays of Italian jewellery, pottery, shoes, and clothes to be rented for weddings. She resolutely walks past without buying. "Every time I got ten dollars I put in bank," she says. "I do without many things till I go and bring back what I got in Italia."

Alda's only extravagance is fashion magazines. From newsstands well stocked with Italian publications, she occasionally buys a copy of *Confezioni*, *Annabella*, or *Grazia*, and at her kitchen table she feasts her eyes on the glamorous fashions of Florence, Rome, and Milan, wishing she had more scope for her skill as a dressmaker.

She makes clothes for the children. Last year she tailored a coat for herself and made a jumper with pockets and brass buttons. "I got only one dress I can wear for going out," she laments. "But what's use for more, I go no place where I need. I make dress for Marina and Sylvia, my friends, but I don't put out the sign because nobody want to pay more than two dollars. Bruno say if I work for nothing I better not."

The Pillis' existence follows a monotonous routine. Bruno and Francesco Lutano, their boarder, get up every morning at six-thirty, drink black coffee, and take a streetcar to work. Alda gets up an hour later, gives the children milk and an egg, sends Luigi to school, and while she does her housework, looks after Paulo and two-year-old Maria who belongs to the family upstairs. When Bruno gets home from his job he goes to the basement, takes a shower, and comes up to the kitchen shining and hungry.

Bruno, Francesco, and the children sit round the table, and in front of each Alda puts a great plate of spaghetti covered with sauce she has made of tomatoes, garlic, and olive oil, sprinkled with Parmesan cheese. "Spaghetti makes man strong," she says. "Fills him up; he like every day very much."

Alda then gives them meat, mashed potatoes, a green salad dressed with lemon and olive oil, or a vegetable – cauliflower, eggplant, or broccoli dipped in a batter and fried golden brown. The meat is usually thin slices of fried veal or boiled chicken. "We not used to beef – in Italy is very tough," Alda tells me. "Here we have meat every day; in Italy can afford only three times a week."

On Sunday Alda gives her family pizza. She runs round to the Roma Bakery and for twenty cents buys a loaf-sized piece of dough that is ready to be pulled into an olive-oiled pan and dotted with anchovies, olives, and tomato sauce.

For dessert there is always fresh fruit; sometimes there is cake, or bread and gorgonzola or zombrosi cheese, followed by coffee. With their meal the Pillis drink wine made by Bruno with grapes from California (he says Canadian grapes are not sweet enough). Paulo and Luigi drink milk or a little wine in a glassful of water.

After dinner Alda spends most of the evening washing and scouring the dishes, filling the lunch boxes of the men, and getting the children into bed. Bruno repairs leaky plumbing, works in the basement or garden, or sits at the kitchen table with a bottle of beer and Francesco or anyone who might have dropped in. When there is an Italian program on their tiny radio or an Italian film on TV they give it their casual attention. Bedtime for the family is usually ten o'clock. But not for Francesco – he goes to the shows and to dances.

There are several Italian clubs in Little Italy where the members play cards and dance. Bruno doesn't belong to them because he is saving his money. Nor does he take his family to the Italian Gardens, a park in North Toronto, where for a fee people can picnic, play *bocce* or *scopa*, listen to music, and chat with their friends. Only once Bruno yielded to the temptation of being one of the throngs of Italians that fill Massey Hall when there is an entertainer from Italy.

Though they are very friendly and generous, the Pillis have little social life; they don't know many people in their part of Toronto. Most Italians of Little Italy come from Calabria (the toe of Italy) or from the island of Sicily; many of them cling to their traditions and keep to themselves. A priest of the district says, "They are a different kind of soup from the Italians who live north of Rome" – like the Pillis, who come from the proud northern province of Tuscany.

Alda does not know her neighbours. Those on one side of the triplex come from Abruzzi. "Abruzzi people nice but don't talk," Alda says. Those on the other side are from Calabria. "On some days say good morning, good evening; next day say nothing. People from Toscano talk much." Alda laughs. "We like to talk."

Most of the northern Italians in Toronto live north of Little Italy, and among them Alda and Bruno have friends who teasingly ask why the Pillis don't move out of the ghetto. "Because it is cheaper there," Bruno tells them. "We want to save money to build our own home and live private."

Marina and Guido live north. They have a car, a house, and three children. They and the Pillis exchange visits about once a month. Marina says Alda is her best friend in Canada. "If I sick she look after my kids." Marina, from Treviso, is bouncy, jolly, and generous; as soon as the Pillis arrive at her house she gives them coffee with a spurt of whisky to flavour it; she puts a batch of Italian records on the hi-fi, then passes cake and liqueur. The men dance gaily with their wives – for a moment – then go to the basement and play *scopa* with other friends of Guido, who always seem to be there. The women talk about their children and clothes. Marina tells Alda she is learning much English from a Canadian woman next door; Alda tells Marina the Calabrian man next door to her slapped Luigi for going into his garden after a ball; Luigi's face bled, was swollen and bruised, and she called the police.

Luigi says he has eleven friends: Mario, two Tonys, two Guiseppis, two Pasqualles, Joe, Leslie, Dominic, and Francesco; they are all in his class at school. They never come to his house. He plays with them in the alley and parking lot. They play ball and hide-and-seek, and they enact the thrillers and westerns they have seen on TV.

In winter Luigi spends most of his time after school on the floor of the bedroom watching television with Paulo. In summer Alda and Bruno or Francesco sometimes take the children to play in High Park; on a Sunday Alda packs food for a picnic and they go by streetcar and ferry to Toronto Island and sit on the sand.

Bruno takes no holidays. "He work all the time." Alda sighs. "With no car, holiday is no good." Alda and the children have seen nothing of Canada beyond the congested heart of Toronto except on one memorable day when Bruno rented a car and took his family to view the world marvel they'd heard of in Italy: Niagara Falls.

"If I have much money I buy Canadian car and we do much travel." Bruno grins.

"We could go for walk in car every Sunday." Alda's eyes shine at the prospect.

"But first we got to have house, not big house, just for four," Bruno reminds her.

"And maybe little girl baby when we come back from trip to Italia," Alda dreams.

"Then we have two born in Canada." Bruno laughs.

"Why didn't you born me in Canada?" Luigi wants to know. "I want to be a Canadian."

"You are Canadian." Alda smiles at her son who has crew-cut hair and is wearing a plaid shirt and blue jeans.

"Then why do I talk Italian?" Luigi asks her.

"So you can talk to your father and me and teach us to talk English."

Most of the English Alda speaks she has learned from Luigi, who, though only in grade two at school, has the responsibility of interpreting for the whole family.

"What means pretty?" Alda asks him. Bruno, trying to read a typed letter, wants to know what are the little hooks printed before a word. They laugh when Francesco asks for more soap and means soup. Alda says, "I get always wrong, kitchen and chicken." Bruno asks, "And why is dad and dead said the same but mean different?"

Little Paulo shouts, "Look me, look me." He often runs to his father and says, "Stick 'em up," or "Give's a kiss, Bobbo." Sometimes he says it in English, sometimes in Italian.

"He learns very good from TV," Bruno says, fondly embracing his little son.

Bruno once enrolled in an English course at night school but he was so tired after long hours of using a pick and shovel at his job that he fell asleep in the class and soon gave it up.

Francesco has a little grammar book, which he often brings to the Pillis' kitchen to ask Luigi for the explanation of a phrase. Francesco believes his inability to master English in the two years he's been here has marked him as stupid. Though he has a mechanic's diploma he is paid only $2.10 an hour, instead of the much higher rate he should get. Despite this, Francesco declares happily that he loves his job and Canada is the land of his dreams.

Bruno has no desire now to go back to Italy except for a visit. Even Alda, though lonely, says she would rather keep living in Canada. "Is better here for Luigi and Paulo to get education. I want them go to high school and be maybe electrician or plumber, be something that they got a trade and can work all the time. Not to be labourer; labour is cheap, always first out of job."

"I want to have a gun and be a policeman." Luigi takes the stance of a gunman and points a finger at Paulo.

"What you be when you a man, Paulo?" Francesco asks.

Paulo shouts, "Big," and they laugh.

"Go to school and learn good to read," Bruno says, "that's how to be man."

"But you can't read English good, Bobbo."

"Bruno learn," Alda says confidently. "Every day a little bit. By time Edna have story in book Bruno know how to read it."

Bruno looks modest. "I learn. In summer I get Canadian citizenship," he says. "Then we all be Canadian."

"Hurray! Hurray!" shouts Luigi.

"Ray! Ray! Ray!" Paulo echoes.

Alda says, "When Bruno build little house we have it like Marina beside Canadian family and learn very fast how speak and do all things Canadian."

"Mmm, Canadian-style cooking." Luigi rolls his brown eyes. "Hamburgers, hot dogs, potato chips, Cokes."

"Chewie gum," Paulo adds and rolls his eyes too.

"Canada better place to live in than Italy," Bruno says, "but I still like best how my wife cook: spaghetti, pizza, *radicchio*, lasagne."

"And *vino* is better for drink than Canadian rye whisk." Francesco beams.

Alda smiles and fondly agrees.

Chatelaine, March, 1965

☆　☆　☆　☆　☆

Before my story about Alda and Bruno appeared in *Chatelaine* in 1965 the Pilli family had gone back to Italy for a visit and stayed there. The following year, on a trip to Italy, I went to the ancient walled city of Lucca, where the concierge of my hotel phoned a pub in the Pillis' native village, and I was told exactly how I could find them in their new home in Via Reggio. I went there on a bus.

With pride they showed me their pleasant little house in the suburbs of the charming seaside town. "Much more nice, you think?" Alda asked me wistfully. "Toronto place not good." I heartily agreed.

Bruno was again driving a truck, carrying marble from Cararra through the mountains. "Now I worry again," Alda told me, "such dangerous work, but good living here." She seemed to be always smiling.

Luigi and Paulo played with friends in their grassy walled yard. Luigi refused to speak to me. "Won't speak English," Alda said. "He speaks now only Italian, like other kids." But while we were having dinner and Alda groped for an English word, Luigi immediately supplied it – then shyly hung his head. "He knows, you see, he knows," Alda cried, "but won't speak."

Afterword

A journalist friend once said to me, "Edna, why do you spend so much time doing research on the people you write about? I simply make a long list of questions, get all the answers in an hour or two, then come home and write my piece."

I didn't dispute her method but I couldn't work that way. For me it presupposed too much, merely got answers to something already half-known; there was no place for surprises and all those delightful things that happen when you become friends with people, and they are natural in your presence and you learn from them by living their lives with them until you feel you have assimilated enough to write an understanding piece about them.

Then you go home and agonize. You read over your notes and you think and think and think: how to write honestly what you have learned, in such a way that you won't hurt or betray the people who have trusted you and become fond of you. Sometimes it takes weeks, sometimes months for the story to come through.

And when it is written, and edited, and published, there might still be mistakes and hurt feelings, and regrets. But you hope always that the story may have done something to increase someone's understanding – perhaps only your own. Amen.